CAPITAL AND AFFECTS

SEMIOTEXT(E) FOREIGN AGENTS SERIES

Originally published as *Il posto dei calzini. La svolta linguistica dell'economia e i suoi effetti nella politica.* © 1994 Edizioni Casagrande.
© This edition 2011 by Semiotext(e).

Published by Semiotext(e)
2007 Wilshire Blvd., Suite 427, Los Angeles, CA 90057
www.semiotexte.com

Special thanks to John Ebert and Marc Lowenthal.

Cover art by Josef Strau, *Untitled*, 2008
Drawing, pearls and text on canvas
Courtesy of the artist and Greene Naftali Gallery

Back Cover Photography:
Design by Hedi El Kholti

ISBN: 978-1-58435-103-0
Distributed by The MIT Press, Cambridge, Mass. and London, England
Printed in the United States of America

CAPITAL AND AFFECTS

THE POLITICS OF THE LANGUAGE ECONOMY

Christian Marazzi

Translated and with an Introduction by Giuseppina Mecchia

\<e\>

Contents

Introduction

The work of Italian post-workerist thinkers came to public attention in the English-speaking world after the publication of Michael Hardt's and Antonio Negri's *Empire* (Harvard University Press, 2000). It was long overdue.[1] A native of Ticino, an Italian-speaking canton of Switzerland, Christian Marazzi belongs to the younger generation of Italian autonomists, like his friend and contemporary Franco "Bifo" Berardi. Antonio Negri was his former professor. In the early 1980s, Marazzi left Italy, lived in New York for a few years and studied political economy at the London School of Economics, but he remained close to other Italian economists in exile, Andrea Fumagalli, Antonella Corsani and Carlo Vercellone, with whom he often collaborated over the years. He presently teaches social research at the Universita' della Svizzera Italiana.

First published in Switzerland in 1994 (and revised in 1999 for its first Italian edition) *Capital and Affects* [the original title is "The Place for the Socks"] is already considered a small "classic," and has become an essential reference for many thinkers involved in the critique of contemporary capitalism. It may appear paradoxical that Marazzi's first, most seminal work, would only be translated into English after the publication of two subsequent books of his[2] but, like all real classics, *Capital and Affects* needed to create its own audience by word of mouth and circulate among like-minded intellectuals before reaching a wider audience. When it comes to translation we know that—in keeping with the new economy's requirements—the demand always precedes the offer.

There are more pressing reasons. The economic crisis of 1992, which is powerfully analyzed in the present book, wasn't yet perceived at the time as the symptom of a "systemic" economic mutation. The "dot com" crisis of 2000, and especially the financial crisis of 2008 convinced even the staunchest defenders of capitalism that something might be amiss. Marazzi's recent pamphlet, *The Violence of Financial Capitalism* (Semiotext(e), 2008—new edition 2011), written in the throws of the global meltdown, provided crucial tools that allow us to understand the financial crisis as an important component of capital accumulation rather than as the implosive result of a lack of economic expansion.

1. New Economy, New Exploitation

The transition from Fordism to post-Fordism implemented during Bill Clinton's first term as president was a real turning point. The crisis of 1991–92, with its high rates of unemployment and credit difficulties, and the irreversible losses in industrial and agricultural employment, pointed to a systemic change in production. What was giving value in capital no longer was physical work, but linguistic abilities. Language was becoming a primary factor in the production of goods and in the way they acquired economic value. Both had become fundamental not only in terms of the production process, but also in its "realization," the monetization of the surplus value.

In the early 1990s, Marazzi showed specifically how the reliance on communication was a fundamental tool in the creation of the so-called "just-in-time" production: thanks to increasingly complex communicative instruments, goods and services no longer were offered to the public, they actually preceded the demand. The originality of Marazzi's work, in this book as well as in the following ones, resides in his unique ability to account for the practices that constitute the current forms of value creation and exploitation without presenting them as either justifiable or inevitable. Most of his sources, especially in the first two chapters of this book, are mainstream economists and business leaders thoroughly embedded in the capitalist economy. From the management "guru" Peter Drucker to Intel CEO Andy Grove, and a then little-known Paul Krugman to a not-yet-compromised Paul Romer, the reader of *Capital and Affects* is presented with a rather familiar cast of characters, and not one usually associated with a radical critique of contemporary capitalism. As Michael Hardt wrote in his introduction to *Capital and Language*, "Rare enough are those economists who can communicate to a general public the complexities of financial markets and economic policy. Christian Marazzi is of an even rarer breed of economist who is also able to engage and advance the most exciting veins of contemporary political and social theory." (Marazzi, 2008, 7)

The new crises of the capitalist mode of accumulation are not rare and unpredictable events, they are inherent to the way it works. In fact, as *Capital and Affects* suggests, in an increasingly "communicative"—today we would say "connected"—environment, economic cycles have become remarkably shorter and more far-reaching, since all imbalances in the process of monetarization are immediately registered on a global scale. If, as Paul Virilio already asserted in the late 1970s, speed is the major force of cultural and social change in contemporary societies, this is even truer of economic matters, where information is now transmitted through complex technical systems that go faster than the human brain.[3]

Technical and financial innovation have brought drastic changes in labor management. As a result, the workforce had to adapt to the increasingly volatile process of value creation. Temporary employment, and endemic unemployment, now have become a systemic feature of contemporary capitalist organization. The social imperative to constantly "reinvent oneself" is now part and parcel of the new forms of human exploitation. *Capital and Affects* is among the very first essays in which these mechanisms were identified: socially, they created an ever-widening gap between the rich and the poor, both nationally and internationally; politically, they initiated a frightening erosion of the public sphere, which made the term "middle class" increasingly meaningless. In a recent book, Franco "Bifo" Berardi remarked that the psychological price paid by the individual in this new techno-economical configuration is very high: "The soul, once wandering and unpredictable, must now follow functional paths in order to become compatible with the system of operative exchanges structuring the productive ensemble… Industrial factories used the body, forcing it to leave the soul outside of the assembly line… The immaterial factory asks instead to place our very souls at its disposal: intelligence, sensibility, creativity and language."[4]

For the last three years, *The New York Times* and other newspapers have been publishing heart-breaking stories featuring the plight of the new poor, former inhabitants of the American suburban dream newly ruined by unemployment, healthcare emergencies and crushing debt. Harrowing stories of foreclosures, urban blight, crumbling infrastructures and public deficits have become the object of political bickering between so-called "fiscal conservatives" and "liberal spendthrifts." Amidst this mindless pathos, the lucid and informed analysis provided by *Capital and Affects* is a powerful reminder of the way we got ourselves into this situation in the first place.

In the early 1990s, when *Capital and Affects* was originally written, much pride and optimism was tied to working in certain sectors of this economy, mostly in software design and management. The exploitative nature of the relation between capital and the mental and affective capacities of these new "serfs" was largely hidden by the feeling of being on the "cutting edge" of the new economy. Since then, the "dot com" bust and the off-shoring of informational labor have delivered a substantial blow to this sense of self-worth, and the information workers are now feeling a little closer to their degraded "immaterial" companions, the people working in the care and hospitality sectors and mainly involved with the creation of corporate, social and affective relations. After the financial crisis of 2007–2008, even management has lost much of its luster as it became clear that if there is nothing to manage, no manager is required any longer. In today's labor market, the realities of contemporary forms of exploitation are becoming much more difficult to ignore.

Marazzi's emphasis on the capitalist valorization of linguistic processes, and therefore of the most fundamental form of our mental activity, also alerts us to the flattening that is occurring in the intellectual field as they are being subtracted from the common space of love and knowledge and recirculated in distorted and manipulated forms. As Deleuze and Guattari pointed out only a few years before, "if the three ages of the concept are the encyclopedia, pedagogy, and commercial professional training, only the second can safeguard us from falling from the heights of the first into the disaster of the third."[5] Christian Marazzi's work should probably be read as an example of the kind of pedagogy that is needed right now as we are trying to find new, less inequitable ways to occupy the contemporary social landscape.

2. New Exploitation, New Struggles

Christian Marazzi isn't outwardly critical of the developments that he so cogently describes both in *Capital and Affects* and in his later books. It would be a mistake, however, to infer from it that he has relinquished his political commitment in order to analyze the instruments of power. Pedagogy is a step forward with respect to pure scholarship, as it always implies a space of public intervention. And, in fact, the impetus motivating all of Marazzi's economic investigations is first and foremost political. Sketching the contours of possible interventions, he addresses two levels of organization and institution that have been widely debated during the last decade. Locally, he examines diverse forms of community initiatives taken independently from macro-institutions, for instance programs meant to reinsert drug-addicts in Swiss urban neighborhoods. Reclaiming Antonio Gramsci's notion of a "civil society," he shows how limited, decentralized and transversal forms of social citizenship are necessary to offset the fragmentation of public space resulting from current forms of capitalist exploitation. The only antidote to "lean production" is, indeed, "lean organization" on the part of the exploited. Globally, experience shows that governments only respond to a sustained and ultimately independent social action.

One cannot reverse a mode of production, only a political regime. At a time when political regimes are being hollowed out by the imperatives of economic valorization, it is strategically preferable to implement minoritarian, marginal forms of socio-economic organization in order to counter, at least in part, the systemic drive toward wealth disparity and social impoverishment. In the introduction to his forthcoming book, *The Communism of Capital* (forthcoming, Semiotext(e)), Marazzi elaborates on the political agenda which concludes *Capital and Affects*: "Our objective is clear: impose collectively, and from the bottom up, new rules for the financial markets; invest in public services, education and welfare; create public employment in the new energy sector; refuse the de-fiscalization of high revenues; reclaim the right to a job and a social income; build spaces for self-determination."[6] The present book was written in the mid-1990s. What was prescient then has now become our present socio-economic reality.

— Giuseppina Mecchia

Prologue

We do little more than state the obvious when, trying to come to terms with the politico-institutional earthquakes traversing our times, we say that language is the key to politics. What is less evident is how to locate the present political transformations within the new modes of production, the technologies that are reshaping the production of goods and services, and the work relations structuring our daily life. Whether we like it or not, the entry of communication—and therefore of language—in the sphere of production is at the very origin of the epochal turn characterizing the present. The paradigmatic shift that we are trying to describe in the following pages—the transition from fordism to post-fordism, from mass production and consumption to the flexible production and distribution systems commonly called *just in time*[1]—forces our analysis to go beyond the disciplinary boundaries established by the organization of knowledge typical of the last decade. What is at stake is not only the understanding of our world, but our very being in this world.

Our first chapter is a general presentation of the different aspects contributing to the definition of the post-fordist social model, which is constituting itself in the wake of the communication technologies and techniques typical of the so-called "information societies." Our second chapter analyzes the upheavals brought about by the socioeconomic crisis and the spaces of conflict that it creates. In the third chapter, we formulate several hypotheses concerning the redefinition of the relation between State and markets in the age of economic globalization.

This book finds its roots in a sense of political urgency tied to a larger existential unease. Transition times are tragic: we only see the outlines of the new, while still subject to the limits of the old. We stumble forward between these two extremes.

When we feel lonely, deprived of the analytic categories that would tell us where we are actually going, what keeps us going and encourages us in our research are the people, the images and the relationships dearest to us: this book is dedicated to my sister Giovanna.

1

Starting from Work

1. Lean Production

The current economic recession[1] occurred during an ongoing
transformative crisis in the modes of social production, consumption and communication. This makes an analysis of the "epochal
shift" characteristic of our time even more difficult. When we hear
that the economic engine is finally recovering after two or three years
of crisis because we are finally seeing a rise in employment figures,
we have to be very careful. It is easy to say that new jobs are being
created or that the construction business is picking up and exports
and consumption are rising, but assessing the irreversible changes
in the *nature* of work and of social rights that happened before,
during and after the recession is quite another matter.

A recession is a phase of what we call an *economic cycle*, an
oscillatory (or palindromic) movement that perpetuates itself by
swinging between two insurmountable limits. "By a cyclical movement we mean that as the system progresses in, e.g, the upward
direction, the forces propelling it upwards at first gather force and
have a cumulative effect on one another but gradually lose their
strength until at a certain point they tend to be replaced by forces
operating in the opposite direction." This is how John Maynard

Keynes defined the rationality of the economic cycle, and he added, "We mean also that there is some recognizable degree of regularity in the time-sequence and duration of the upward and downward movements."[2]

During the 1980s and the beginning of the 1990s we have observed a modification when measuring the periodicity and the duration of the economic cycle. While during the post-war era the average duration of the cycle was five years, after the international recession of 1980–1981 ten years passed before the explosion of the following recession. Not only has the distance between the two recessions become longer (from five to ten years), but the duration of the recession itself seems definitely longer than the preceding ones. After three years of recession and several signs of recovery notwithstanding, there is still much confusion among economists with regard to the end of the recession. People talk of a "timid," "anemic" recovery, and the monetary authorities forecast high and unpredictable inflation rates, at least in the short term. Even the new jobs don't make up for the ones lost during the recession, and for the most part they are not of very high quality.

These changes in the economic cycle, in its duration and—as we will see later—in the different factors determining the interaction between occupation, income, inflation and interest rates, are the symptoms of a much deeper *crisis-transformation* in our societies. In other words, the economic cycle has changed because the advanced economies are traversed by restructuring forces that are working beyond the cycle's rationality. If we want to understand the dynamics and the form of the new economic cycle and in order to anticipate its moves, we need to start from an analysis of these underlying changes.

We know that the unprecedented layoffs of these last few years, which introduced the phenomenon of mass unemployment even in a country like Switzerland,[3] were aimed at the reduction of labor costs in both the public and the private sectors. Such costs were considered excessive in an increasingly global economic context, which is constantly subject to the pressures of international competition. This is what has been called *lean production*. We know that, in order to reduce the weight of social benefits held responsible for high labor costs, many companies chose to shed entire segments of production by *outsourcing* them. With this term we indicate the recourse to contractors, consultants and former employees, in order to increase the productivity and efficacy of larger firms. This implies a radical restructuring of the firm's organization. This also means that big corporations, government agencies, large hospitals and universities will no longer be the sole employers of large numbers of people. This is why, while the large firms are laying off people, the small and medium companies working for them are in fact the only forces able to create employment, although this is often precarious in nature. More generally, the large employers will increasingly tie occupation to results, while the rest of the work will be contracted to other companies.[4]

This is lean production, then, and the outsourcing of social costs through the hiring of subcontractors. To take just an example, we could think about the recourse to private cleaning companies in hospitals or in public offices, but things go deeper than that. Big companies are reorganizing themselves with new technologies, in order to respond to shifts in demand and to the changing taste and desires of the client-consumers in a very short time. We are talking of "just-in-time" production, which organizes labor in the most flexible way possible, thus avoiding the accumulation of stock (that is, unsold merchandise that is destined to depreciate itself). This is clearly the most visible aspect that differentiates the emerging mode of production from the preceding one, the era following the First World War which has been called "Fordist." This name, of course, is derived from the American industrialist Henry Ford, who at the beginning of the 20th Century first introduced the assembly line in his automobile factories. While during Fordism the times and modes of production were rigidly planned, in the post-Fordist era planning is much harder, since one has to rely much more on the opportunities offered by the market. These opportunities have to be seized upon immediately because in periods of strong competition and markets' oversaturation even the smallest change in demand can make or break a company's balance sheets.

The passage from Fordism to post-Fordism, from planned production to a production increasingly driven by the market's every whim, has to be analyzed with great attention. This is where the most important changes actually reside.

In the study of the most distinctive traits of what we call "lean production," or "just-in-time," with respect to the Fordist mode of production, the most useful is certainly the one that sees in *communication processes* the crux of today's social and political transformations. We can say that lean production has brought communication, or the flow of information, directly into the production processes. In this new mode of production, communication and production overlap, while in the Fordist mode of production they were juxtaposed.

There is no mystery in communication's new role: when confronted with an oversaturated market, due to a limited buying power on the part of consumers and therefore of the market's ability to absorb excess production, the mode of production had to adjust and restructure itself in order to increase productivity without creating excess inventory. Productivity gains no longer happen within "economies of scale," which, in Fordism, were created by increasing the quantity of produced goods (thereby reducing their unit price), but they are tied to the production of small quantities of many different products, reducing to zero defective output and immediately responding to the market's oscillations.

The factory has necessarily become "minimalist," in the sense that everything that exceeds the market's demand has to be eliminated. People have also talked about "zero-stock" strategies, because as soon as one sees an increase in unsold merchandise there is a prompt intervention to eliminate the causes of overproduction, whether it means getting rid of workers or of machinery. What is important is the elimination of all redundancy with respect to the demand, the cutting out of all the "grease" accumulated during the working process.

One understands, then, how communication—and its productive organization as information flow—has become as important as electricity once was in the age of mechanical production. In fact, communication is the grease that insures the smooth running of the entire production process, from the sale and distribution to the production stage. Communication, in fact, allows us to realize *the reversal* of the relation between production and consumption,[5] offer and demand, and that forces a structuring of the productive process in the most flexible way possible, breaking all the rigidities constituted by the employees' working habits.

From a distribution point of view, with its strategic function in regulating the productive process, the introduction of optical scanners at supermarket checkouts, which read the information contained in the barcodes of all kinds of products, represents one example of the reversal between offer and demand, production and consumption. Optical scanners are formidable information collectors with respect to all the data relative to retail sales, in regard to quantity, periods (and even hours) of bigger consumption, or a product's "direct profitability" in terms of floor space, packaging, color, etc. In the same manner, the opportunity to pay with credit cards has made of the sale and distribution stage the place for collecting all sorts of useful data regarding the consumer, which allows the personalization (or "singularization") of the mass consumption of goods and services.[6]

When applied to the sphere of distribution, information technology has granted more power to the large distribution outlets with respect to the producers of goods, precisely because of their strategic position in the collection of information vital to the control not only of the promotion of a certain product, but also of its "life cycle." Retail outlets, having acquired the control of the data flows derived from their customers, are now in the position to determine the times and the quantities of merchandise produced. In the new, post-Fordist system, *effective* sales directly "command" orders and, therefore, production.

From the point of view of production, the most spectacular changes in work organization with respect to the Fordist era are also a function of communication processes.[7] An almost emblematic expression of this new orientation is the *Kan-Ban*, which consists in placing on shipping cards a kind of tag that serve both as order requests and delivery notifications. The *Kan-Ban* is a mechanism that coordinates different working positions thanks to an information flow that moves horizontally in a back-and-forward motion, without any need for central planning.

In Fordism, daily, monthly or annual planning was determined in offices that were kept separate from direct operations, and the workflow proceeded from the first stage of production to the last. In the new system, planning is in fact determined by the last stage, that is, by the observation of the market's response, and the entire workflow is organized starting from the information concerning the quantity of goods that need to be produced.

Communication and production overlap, and in fact they are now one and the same. In Fordism communication excluded production and the assembly line was silent, mechanically executing the directions established by the white collar managers. Now, however, in post-Fordism, we have a "speaking," "communicating" production process, and the technologies used in this system can be considered true "linguistic machines," whose main focus is to facilitate and accelerate the circulation of data.

In Fordism, communication in the space of production was considered a destabilizing disruption that could in fact stop production. Either you worked silently or, if you needed to communicate, you had to stop the production process. In the post-Fordist system, instead, the inclusion of communication has a directly productive value.[8]

The working process can't but be deeply conditioned by the entry into production of communication processes. It has to become as flexible as possible, its structure has to be lithe and, most of all, its work force needs to be multivalent, able to move from one task to the next, from one machine to the next without hesitations. The space of production has to insure a maximum of visibility—we need to work in a "shop window"—in order to avoid all objective or subjective interruption in the production flow and to capture all circulating information at the right moment.

Once again, the qualitative difference with respect to the Fordist way of working is worth noting. While in Fordism, according to Taylor's injunction, there was the need for a specialized work force, parceled to the point of repeating the same movement all day long, in post-Fordism the "ideal" work force has a high degree of adaptability, in response to changes in rhythm and function. This has to be a multi-operational work force, able to "read" the information flows and *to work while communicating*. Post-Fordist work implies a re-association of formerly clearly distinct functions, a "reconfiguration" of a whole series of executive roles in the person of one individual worker. The Americans call this process *reeingeneering*.[9]

However, one should not spend too much time describing the specifities of post-Fordist organizational models. In fact, there are several of them, and at least up to now none of them has been universally adopted.[10] What is crucial is the understanding that at the basis of the radical transformation in the post-Fordist mode of production there is the merging of production and communication, of "instrumental" and "communicative" actions—if we want to use expressions coming from the realm of philosophy. Communication's entry into a "talking" production, which uses linguistic machines whose importance resides much more in their data-collection abilities (software) than in their physical configuration (hardware) or their value as fixed capital, is the historic consequence of the crisis in the classic relationship between the spheres of production and distribution.

Once the market is oversaturated, either because the classic goods that made the history of Fordism—such as cars or house appliances—are by now "mature" products whose quantitative distribution is reaching its limit, or because the purchasing power of the consumer population is stagnant or even diminishing, the production process needs to be revolutionized. From now on, it will no longer be possible to produce large quantities of highly standardized goods, nor to accumulate inventories thinking that they will eventually sell at some future, non entirely predictable moment (what during Fordism was called "just-in-case" production). It won't be possible to produce according to "economies of scale." Instead, we will need to produce limited amounts of differentiated goods, which will vary according to the changing "taste" of consumers that we will need to know as well as possible in order to better reach them, while at the same time trying to find the best ways to realize gains in productivity.

2. Japanese Origins

Post-Fordist production and distribution models were born in Japan in the 1950s in the Toyota factories (hence the term *Toyotism*, often used to characterize lean production). This can be explained by the socioeconomic specificities of Japan during that period, among which we need to mention at least two. The first characteristic was a limited market that made it impossible to simply adopt the already proven American techniques for mass production, which presupposed a mass consumption or, at least, a foreseeable expansion.[11] The gradual introduction of toyotism from Japan to the Western economies in fact follows the production and consumption crisis that started with the 1974–1975 recession (the oil crisis that marked the beginning of the first austerity policies) and continued with the adoption of the neoliberal policies of the 1980s.

The second reason for the Japanese birth of post-Fordism is also, although only in part, related to the specific characteristics of the Japanese economy. The origins of the working revolution in Toyota's factories can be found in a financial crisis (1949), a major strike (1950) and the Korean War (1950–1953). The financial crisis suffered by Toyota in 1949 was the consequence of the austerity policies adopted by the Japanese government in 1948, which caused a decline in demand and thence a sale crisis for Toyota products. Toyota's financial crisis, in turn, will force it to resort to a bank consortium that will impose on the company a drastic reduction in work force and the planning of production in direct relation with actual sales.

The 1950 strike, like the ones that followed in 1952 and 1953, will be the last attempt at resistance on the part of a working class organized in professional trade unions. The losses suffered in those years sanctioned the shift from professional trade unions to unions internal to the firm. This shift, that marked the irreversible crisis of professional trade unions, also sanctioned the destruction of a working class which, up to that moment, was organized in larger trade unions in order to counter industrial "rationalization" and wage reductions. The destruction of this working class was necessary to the introduction of the new production methods introduced by Mr. Ohno, who in fact was the Japanese incarnation of Taylor, the original theoretician of lean production. With this aim in mind, what needed to be created was a working class strongly implied in the entrepreneurial spirit, faithful to the firm's objectives, capable of adapting to its imperatives and ready to identify with its destiny. This was particularly true during the Korean War, when Toyota found itself in the paradoxical situation of having to respond to a surge in demand on the part of the United States without being able to implement new hires.

It is not difficult to see in these historical circumstances the reasons that explain the spread of Toyotism in the West during the following decades. During the 1980s, neoliberal policies in fact reduced the market's ability to absorb production, due to the fall in real wages and the compression of the State's social expenditures. Culturally, though, the Fordist model in the West was already in crisis, following the international cycle of struggles that had started in 1968: central to these struggles was the critique of the exploitation of mass workers, accompanied by the demand for an education that would provide an alternative to a life sentence to be served on the factory floors.

During the social, economic and political crisis of the 1970s, the production and organization models of Fordism start to wane, but no less important is the crisis of the social and cultural models on which they rested. The parceling of production in micro-firms, the concept of "technological frugality" espoused by the burgeoning ecologist movement (the "small is beautiful" philosophy typical of the 1970s), the organization of a more intellectual kind of work, the "refusal" of salaried work as form of life, will all progressively contribute to the construction of a new paradigm of production and development.

3. Innovation and Political Forms

The passage from Fordism to post-Fordism brings new life to the research about how to periodize the diffusion of industrial techniques, technologies and organizational models, which have always been the object of historical inquiry. Certainly, it confirms the thesis according to which technical innovation and invention cannot explain, in and by themselves, truly epochal socioeconomic transformations. No technical consideration could explain why what was applied in Japan during the 1950s had to wait almost thirty years to find its way West.

In this respect, there exist many historical precedents.[12] The classic example is the mechanical harverster: its invention goes back to 1780, but its usage was generalized only eighty years later, during the American Civil War, because of the sudden lack of agricultural workers. The traumatic change in living conditions and social relations caused by the war was essential to the beginning of an agricultural innovation process which, in only three decades, radically revolutionized the oldest among all socialized productive activities. The harvest, with its employment of a large work force, had been not only a necessary activity in an economy mostly based on the production of subsistence goods, but also part of a traditional way of life, of a system of social relations and power distribution which could not be changed without causing social unbalances and political instability.

In other words, we need an external shock, such as a war or a social crisis, in order to create the conditions for applying systems of production and consumption that could not be applied during "normal" times, when social and political compromises can easily be reached. There is no doubt that the 1970s, with their social instability, the crisis in the North/South relations (prices of raw materials), and the waning of Fordist work ethics, did create the conditions for the generalization of a productive and organizational model born not only in a different country, but in a single company. On the other hand, Fordism was also born in Ford's factories, and only later was adopted by all Western economies, and even then not without difficulty and with many changes with respect to the original model. Through the lens of historical analysis, the passage from the single innovative company to the economic system, the institutional passage from micro to macro can at times appear paradoxical. Thus, from the point of view of salaried relations, while toyotism was originally close to the paternalism ideated by Ford in order to manage his company at the beginning of the century, American Fordism will actually evolve *in opposition* to Ford's ideas.[13] The gradual emergence of the collective wage conventions typical of Fordism will be the result of negotiations *between State, trade unions and private employers*, and not at all of the wage paternalism preached by Ford for the single company: *nemo propheta in patria*.

The transition between Fordism and post-Fordism also sheds light on another, not negligible, political and institutional phenomenon. The new technological and organizational "leaps" are not primarily technical in nature, but rather they are the function of vast, "preprogrammed" investments in scientific research. This is accomplished to the transformation of scientific institute, research centers and educational institutions. The issue of the political control exerted on the innovation processes that destroy social circles, routines and preexisting power relations is at the very core of these phenomena. The genius of the innovative entrepreneur, of a leader such as Toyota or Ford that was theorized by the Austrian economist Joseph Schumpeter, is not enough to start a process of generalized social transformation. The single entrepreneur cannot see the political problems derived from the new relation realized in the entrepreneurial act through the convergence of science, research and the sociopolitical regulation of society.[14] The figure of the entrepreneur cannot operate the synthesis between innovative research and the management of imbalances, between the disharmonies inherent to the diffusion of new organizational and productive techniques and the rest of society.

In the passage to post-Fordism, the issue of the relation between entrepreneurship and politics, between the subject of innovation and the political subject, appears in completely new terms. In Fordism, the *separation* between entrepreneurial innovation and the political management of its consequences was founded on the fact that the decisional centers of the two systems were *qualitatively different*. On one side there was the economic-productive sphere with its innovations and reorganizations, and on the other there was the politico-administrative sphere, whose main task was to manage, mediate and regulate the consequences of restructuring processes. There was *one subject* who decided on innovation, and *another* who had to understand its consequences; one instance was in charge of sustaining the innovation process, and the other one had to respond to its consequences on social composition and on the general economical equilibrium; there was *one language* for the innovative entrepreneur, and *another language* for economic administration and for the state's politico-bureaucratic governance.

With the entry into communication of the productive sphere, the separation between entrepreneurship and politics is somehow disrupted. This is at the origins of today's main problem, which is far from being solved: *what is the politico-institutional form typical of the post-Fordist regime?* This is an open, extremely complex question deriving directly from the transformations in the mode of production.

4. Linguistic Machines

When we say that in post-Fordism communication participates in production, that it is an immediately productive factor, we are in fact calling into question *language itself*, which is at the basis of human communication. The coincidence of the communicative and of the productive act in the new paradigm opens a vast array of problems tied to the analysis of language, which is as fascinating as it is complex. The limits of this study do not allow for an exhaustive discussion of the questions posed by communication's entry into production. We can only point to some connections and correlations between the "communicative mode of production" and its possible political consequences.

First of all, let us define the problem. With regard to the Fordist era, we spoke of the separation between the economic world of entrepreneurship and the political system, between institutions and administration, entrepreneurs and politicians, innovation and application. This separation was always pragmatic, and it helped to better define the subject's operational competences, in order then to rank him either among "those who are in business," or "those who are into politics."

Between these two spheres there has always been a relation of reciprocal functionality: the instrumental action of the entrepreneur cannot do without the initiatives of the politician. Even within a single firm, the actions performed by the worker on the production line depend on the corporate planning of the white-collar managers, and vice versa. Since the very beginning of industrial production, the workers have always been asked to give their technical suggestions in order to improve the production process, which led to modifications either in the machinery or in the organization of labor routines. However, the essential point is that the suggestions had to be put in a separate box located on the production floor, as one might do for secret or at least private information exchanged between the single worker and management.

This functional separation, which is historical in nature and changes in time, is at the very origin of the transformations in governance, just because we are dealing with different logics and languages. This is why André Gorz, at the beginning of his study on the metamorphoses of labor, quotes Max Weber's description of the transition between the preindustrial and the industrial mode of production.[15]

Before industrial capitalism, the sphere of production was mostly connected to the sphere of the family and of independent artisanal labor. This determined the times and modes of production. Even the industrialists, when they used home-based laborers, left them a large margin of autonomy with respect to how to organize themselves in their intra-familial relationships in order to complete production. The entrepreneur only appeared at the end of the process.

This form of capitalist organization, rooted in tradition, had its own indisputable rationality. The way of life, the profit margins, the quantity of labor produced, the way to manage the enterprise and the relations between entrepreneur and worker was traditional in nature. These relations dominated the way of conducting business and was subjected to the "spirit" and the ethics of that kind of preindustrial entrepreneur.

Weber explained how, when the entrepreneur decides to increase his business beyond traditional levels, he needs to radically transform the form of his productive organization, instituting the *close factory* and hiring the workers who formerly worked for him in their own homes according to a completely different logic. This is how waged labor was born, and with it a new rationality, the economic rationality in its strictest sense. Weber goes to the point of affirming that capitalist rationality is born from an "irrational element," because from now on the "economic man" chooses to exist as a function of his work, of his enterprise, *and not the contrary.*

Anyway, this will impose itself as the *sole* rationality of capital, while Weber, in his reconstruction of the transition between the preindustrial and the industrial epoch, had actually noticed the existence of a *plurality* of rationalities. That only one rationality may exist, ultimately hinges on how economic rationality governs society, on how it imposes itself over all other *possible* rationalities and forms of life; it hinges on the political form that best organizes itself in order to functionally represent this rationality.

The interaction between industrial labor and the political form that is the foundation of industrial capitalism is examined in detail by Hegel at the beginning of the nineteenth Century.[16] Hegel establishes a logical sequence between Work and Government: first we find work, instrumental action, which is founded on the instrumental relation between the individual and the object that he needs. The world of work is an heterogeneous assembly of people devoted to work, each engaged in his or her own struggle with nature aimed at the satisfaction of his or her individual needs. In this world, where an infinity of human beings "act with a goal" according to the logic of the division and specialization of labor, all activities are silent. Acting with a goal means having an instrument that functions mechanically in order to reach a preestablished result. Communication is in fact a monologue: it goes only in one direction, from the project (or goal) to the final result, the product. Between the project and its realization you have the moment of execution, which is mechanic and silent and where "the end justifies the means."

This is why Hegel places communication outside of all directly productive processes, and therefore establishes a *logical* difference between instrumental and communicative actions. Communication, the "dialogic thread" that runs among consciousnesses forming the basis of a people's "spirit," the collective reflection of subjects engaged in different activities, defines the system, the shell within which a society constructs its social, juridical and institutional relations. In turn, the social and political system, built on the basis of the communicative interaction among individual economic subjects, acts on them *retroactively, re-placing* them—so to speak—in the system. Just as work produced its own society, institutions and governments "by means of communication," so do the latter re-produce the economic subjects in establishing rules, laws, norms, prohibitions and redistributive mechanisms.

Since post-Fordism no longer separates production from communication, but makes of their coincidence the very lever of economic development, the first thing to do is to define the kind of communication, or rather of language, that we are describing. This is the kind of language *that produces organization* within the work sphere, inside the firm. In order to better tie production to the oscillations of the market, the working process is structured in order to maximize the fluidity of the circulation of information and respond in real time to the market's demands. Information, therefore, will use a lithe, agile language whose function is aimed at a precise goal. This will be a *logico-formal* language allowing to start essential working routines at the moment of the transmission of information.

This kind of language needs to be as formal as possible, it has to be composed by symbols, signs and abstract codes, an absolutely necessary condition if it has to elicit an immediate interpretation by all those who work in the same company without the least hesitation. The abstraction and artificiality of this language make for a work force that is continually moving (and rotating from task to task, which is necessary in an extremely precarious job market) to be able to understand it and use it in order to respond to the "orders" communicated by the data.

Beyond being formal (abstract, artificial, completely symbolic), this language also needs to be *logical*, because it is thanks to its rules and grammar that one can use it within the firm (or, in the system of "networked production," in several firms), that is, within a "social community" where one's actions cannot interfere with the others', but on the contrary need to support and enhance them.

Formal-logical language was at the basis of the "linguistic machine" theorized in 1936 by the English mathematician Alan Turing, which is at the origin of today's information technologies.[17] This was a "linguistic" machine for which the most important element is the organization of a grammar whose symbols move on a magnetic "assembly line," moving back and forth between one position and another.

The linguistic organization of the production process doesn't characterize only the "Turing machine" and information technologies. The same management models are inspired by the principles expressed by Alan Turing: their goal is to organize the firm as a "data bank" able to self-determine its actions by virtue of a smooth, fluid, "interfaced" linguistic communication process.[18]

5. Language as Political Technology

Now we can understand why it is fundamental to analyze the political theories that consider language and communication as means to improve and intensify democracy's potential. We are thinking about Jürgen Habermas' theory of "communicative acting,"[19] whose greatest merit consists in locating the great political questions of democracy and freedom on the plane of language.

For Habermas, "communicative action," the recourse to linguistic-discursive mediation, is what allows us to justify and legitimize the governance of society by referring to collective interests and needs, also called *general interest*. Thanks to language, according to the theory of "discursive democracy," we can go beyond the pure given, the simple norm, the merely technical-instrumental element.

Linguistic mediation determines the possibility of a cooperative and consensual search for truth. The language we use contains, according to Habermas, a "substantial rationality" *common* to all human beings, which can emerge through communication in order to improve and organize society.

This substantial rationality is similar to the productive activity of individuals in Hegel: it would precede the communicative act itself, belonging to everyone's "lived world" and—like for Hegel's work products—it would migrate from the private to the social sphere thanks to linguistic communication. Each private "lived world" is socialized by language, communication, dialogue among individuals. This is how, thanks to linguistic communication, different individuals organize the social, political and institutional system without which only the "war of all against all" would exist.

The limits of this work make it impossible to consider all the critical arguments that have been made of this vision in the last twenty years, which many considered excessively formal or naïvely enlightened. However, in the context of our analysis of the political problems raised by the post-Fordist regime, we still need to address some of the questions implicit in Habermas' approach, albeit without necessarily solving them.

Habermas' use of communication theory comes from a remarkable intuition at the time when his research started to work on his project, but it is theoretically insufficient to understanding the origin of our own time. In a 1983 interview, Habermas says that his "linguistic turn" dated to the early 1970s, that is, to the so-called "years of lead," the rise of neoconservative ideology and the ecology movements. In order to avoid falling into post- or anti-modernism, becoming "either hardened conservatives or young and wild conservatives," Habermas engaged in the search for a solution. The theory of "communicative action" looked like an excellent "expedient" to remain in modernity without renouncing modernity's mission.

Habermas' theory finds its strength in its pragmatism, which defines linguistic communication as what it is in a given sociopolitical community. Umberto Eco came to the same conclusion in his introduction to *The Limits of Interpretation*, where he explains his attempt at "pacifying" struggles in the linguistic field as follows:

> But I keep thinking that, within the boundaries of a given language, there is a literal meaning of lexical items and that it is the one to be listed first by dictionaries as well as the one that Everyman would first define when requested to say what a given word means. I thus assume that Everyman would say that a fig is a kind of fruit. No reader-oriented theory can avoid such a constraint. Any act of freedom on the part of the reader can come *after*, not *before*, the acceptance of that constraint.[20]

Also, for Habermas, the language commonly used in democratic societies is *the* language that best allows for communication between different subjects-citizens. The values of liberal societies are shared values, whose interpretation doesn't necessarily refer to objective significations (final truths), but at least *to intersubjective* ones. What really counts is that we use socially shared notions, words and signs, and that the words that we use to communicate be chosen because of the fact that the community recognizes them as true. The pragmatism of Habermas' theory resides in his notion of "socially shared" meanings: politicians from all sides can communicate among themselves, provided that they stick with the "etymological" meaning of their words, the one consolidated with the tradition of liberal democracy. Only later, after a political agreement has been reached, can we look at the different ways of interpreting the words that have allowed the elaboration of laws, and the limits of this freedom will be inscribed in the grammatical rules that will constitute the framework of the "democratic conflict."

In the light of what is happening in the 1990s, the insufficiency of Habermas' theory can hardly be denied. It is a structural insufficiency, located in the *juxtaposition* between the "lived" and the "institutional" world.[21] By themselves, language availability and use don't guarantee the complete expression of one's lived world through language's own filters.[22] If, in fact, language is not something innate like, say, hearing, but a *convention*, an arbitrary and artificial human creation transmitted from one generation to the next, what the newborn inherits is a means of communication which does not belong to him naturally, but is externally imposed.[23]

Language learning in childhood implies an original violence, because it forces us to remain silent on lived experiences for which words do not exist and on the other hand to talk about contents that don't correspond to any experience and to formulate intentions that don't belong to us. If on the one hand language allows man to "enter into History," on the other hand it remains a "filter" that cannot let through the lived world of each human being. As the poet said, "words are sealed prisons for the divine breath, for Truth." Language is by definition a disciplinary structure; it imposes limits and prohibitions to the "lived world." Umberto Galimberti said the following, "Language does not reproduce truth, but rather distorts it, although truth cannot announce itself by any other means than language distortions."[24]

On this issue—the role of language as instrument of socialization—Habermas' approach is lacking because it leads to a voluntarism that can easily turn into political naïveté. It is a mistake to construct a theory (which is by definition a universal notion) of communicative action based on the presupposition that the discursive-communicative dimension of the relations between subjects is an objective fact because "socially shared," a reality independent from any critical reflection. This is a presupposition that can have some validity within a circumscribed and internally homogeneous community, like, for instance, the one formed by scholars working in the same field, or by a political class that has developed a conventional communication code. Habermas' theory, when it claims to have a general value, is only a *robinsonade* transposed on the linguistic plane. And in fact, Robinson speaks English to Friday, without ever wondering whether the servant spoke another language before meeting his master.[25]

The theory of discursive democracy does in fact raise the question of the rules necessary for governing a democracy, but without solving within language the conflicts that language itself determines. A critique of communicative action doesn't mean to step outside the world of politics "depriving ourselves of speech." It simply means—but this "simply" is crucial—to assert that within linguistic mediation the existence of each subject is always conflicted: *it is this conflict that constantly modifies any linguistic presupposition.* According to Habermas, those who criticize the communicative dimension of political action are either "vain exhibitionists" or incurable skeptics: this is due to the fact that his analysis stops at the door of productive action, thereby denying itself the possibility to understand political-institutional changes and the transformation of the conditions determined by the new modes of production.

The merit of Habermas' theory of productive action resides in its limits, which we would not have been able to identify if we hadn't been forced to react to his political proposal that embraces liberal democracy and the laws of the market after the fall of the Socialist states. And in fact, these are the limits which constitute the narrow path of today's excursions in the world of politics.

6. The Short Circuit

The disruptive entry of language in the sphere of production represents a leap in our way of thinking about science, technology and productive work. There have been many studies on the increasing importance of technology and on the mechanization of the world, or on the fact that in a market economy the only conceivable rationality is the economic one, according to which only *instrumental action* really exists.

Instrumental action is not founded on shared values, but on *calculations*, whose elements boil down to measuring the adequacy of the means to an end. These are *rational* calculations, derived from a kind of rationality that excludes value judgments by relegating them to a separate sphere, the sphere of communication, of "parlementarity," of linguistic mediation. As McIntyre said:

"Reason is calculating. It can establish factual truths and mathematical relations, but nothing more. In the field of practice, it can only talk about means. When it comes to ends, reason has to keep silent."[26]

Now that communication has entered into production, the dichotomy between the instrumental and the communicative sphere has been upended. Post-Fordist work is highly communicative and needs a high degree of "linguistic" abilities in order to be productive. This kind of work presupposes the capacity to understand *all kinds* of symbolic action (not only in the field of information technology, but also at the purely sensorial-intuitive level). This means that it is in the production process itself that now resides the ability to generalize, to go beyond the data and instrumental-mechanical action allowed by language.

It becomes clearer, now, why the entry into production of communication causes a crisis in the political forms inherited from Fordism—or at least complicates them. The overlap between instrumental and communicative action and the coincidence of production and communication complicate the institutional passage between individual and collective interests. Representative mediations, such as the party-system, the trade unions, or other groups based on corporatism, class, ethnic and social identification becomes, *ab origine*, increasingly hard. Everyone tends to represent solely him or herself; all that is needed to protect one's own interests is the understanding of the communicative techniques within the working-productive process (*Berlusconi docet*). The entrepreneur, as such, becomes a politician, a subject of governance, leaping over the chasm between economic and political spheres typical of representative democracies. His paradoxical "trustworthiness" and "prestige" derive from being the subject of instrumental and communicative acting *at the same time*. He can lie (in particular when an entire political class is being legally prosecuted) because— in truly Hobbesian fashion—lies are part of the linguistic-communicative arsenal utilized to produce goods and services, especially when these goods are by definition "representational goods," world *images*.[27]

The crisis in social cohesion and the proliferation of political self-representational forms (which, paradoxically, only reveal the qualitative deficit in political representation) derive from the "linguistic turn" that contaminated the sphere of production after having revolutionized the cultural and esthetic realm, the scientific universe and finally, "with Habermas," the political sphere. The currently indispensible function of linguistic mediation in every productive operation determines the absolute need for a political solution and for some form of governing economic activity, but the political solutions that have been proposed seem destined to evanescence. In fact, their short life is probably due to the fact of being *circumscribed* to instrumental action within a single entre-preneurial sector or economic interest.

The difficulty in finding, in the post-Fordist era, a plane of supra-individual mediation for consolidating lasting compromises and agreements comes directly from the short circuit between instrumental and communicative action. In instrumental action, the relation between ends and means is mechanic: once an objective has been determined, and a good needs to be produced in order to maximize one's own profits, the execution of this project is univocal and unilateral. The decision is rational for what concerns the calculation of pros and cons, and even if the calculation is limited, it is still a calculation. All the rest, all other actions, all other behaviors, are not part of the decision but simply irrational reflexes.

Communicative action, on the contrary, is all but straightforward, it does not simply go to the end to the means. Nature, as Einstein noted, is not the univocal text theorized by the scientists belonging to the Newtonian tradition, who thought that the observation of Nature and the deduction of its internal laws was sufficient to find the scientific legality of the physical world. The experience of theoretical inquiry has actually shown that Nature is, rather, an *equivocal* text that can be read according to *alternative modalities*. If on the one hand the internal and external universe does not speak and on the other hand it is us, with our dictionaries, who make it speak, this means that we build multiple visions of the same universe, or even a plurality of worlds theoretically corresponding to the plural subjects who invent them.[28]

The instrumental use of communication creates a friction between instrumental and communicative action, between linear and multidirectional methods, between the One and the multiple. Once the productive objective has been decided, the means and the ends to reach it can be modified along the way, so that at the end of the productive process the result might be quite different from what had been originally planned. This is the root of the difficulty inherent to the construction of a lasting form of government that would allow the determination of rules and norms (no matter how fictitious) for a consensual management of the multiplicity of interests existing in society.

From the certitudes of the former era, we are now in a time of questioning, a state of perpetual interrogation. We keep asking ourselves why the answers to the problems facing us today are not only multiple (which potentially constitutes a formidable enrichment for our lives) but also less and less shared socially and reciprocally convertible. At the peak of the "communication society," we are paradoxically witnessing a *crisis of* communication itself.

The passage from security to precariousness, from planning to fortuities, is therefore inherent to a structural crisis that will last for a very long time. The post-Fordist restructuration has been forced to internalize communication. The danger consists in not being able to see the origin of the crisis experienced by the representative democracies inherited from the Fordist era. The danger also consists in not wanting to redefine our political categories on this basis, refusing to traverse the crisis innovating our analytical instruments, our ways of thinking and the organizational forms of representative democracy that we have inhabited all our lives.

The poet, who literally is a "maker," someone who works with words, had understood it a long time ago. Commenting on Hölderlin, whose poetry is "a destiny for us," Heidegger wrote that "language, the field of 'the most innocent of all occupations,' is also 'the most dangerous' of goods... the danger of all dangers because it first creates the possibility of danger."[29]

7. Servility

One of the "solutions" proposed to the issues raised by the post-Fordist transformation and that, at least for the time being, seems to transform politics by destroying its most basic principles, is to be found in the increasing "servility" of productive labor.

In the new way of working, a high rate of devotion to the company's objective is necessary: those who have the privilege of working in a long-term position have to demonstrate a total availability to the "mood shifts" within the company and to the oscillations in production caused by the variations in demand. This is the explanation for the increase in overtime, often unpaid, which would seem paradoxical when on the outside a full 10 percent of the population is statistically unemployed. This, however, also explains why we are moving from a regime where in the job market the social rights of the workers were almost universally acknowledged (in the form, for instance, of collective bargaining) and were protected by solid and lasting juridical norms, to a regime where workers rights are rapidly disappearing under the pressure of economical needs and contingencies. When the marketing of goods is in charge and imposes quantity and quality in real time (just-in-time), work becomes increasingly constrictive: we need to show ourselves capable of devotion and obedience, under penalty of losing our job. When production can no longer be planned since the market is no longer able to expand infinitely, as happened in Fordism, due to the compression of purchasing power; when, in other words, contingency reigns, the unforeseeable becomes the rule and everything rests on immediate adaptability. The spaces for juridical protections and universal rights, independent from specific juridical persons, close up.

The normative regulation of the job market—which was also a characteristic of Fordism, where even the representatives of conflicting and antagonistic interests were called to cooperate in order to produce norms able to resolve productive problems—is now being replaced by a sort of "*industrial feudality.*" While the plant, the hospital, the office are becoming the place of fidelity, the job market becomes the place of instability, fragmentation and separation in terms of class, sex and race. The job market is now the place of the absence of universal rights. This real transformation of the mode of production finds in its origins the current model of "totalitarian democracy," which is the *democracy without rights* that is staring at us from a totally plausible future. This is democracy without rights because the relation in real time with people's tastes—people who are no longer referred to as "citizens" and thereby as juridical subjects, but as "consumers," "customers" and thereby as subjects of consumption—overcomes any juridical mediation, any appeal to lasting and verifiable norms.[30]

This scenario is dramatically verified in the normative differences between the American, the European and the Japanese job markets. The most recent comparative studies show how in the United States the absence of regulation in working relations and the lack of an efficient system of representation and consultation of salaried workers—in other words the absolute flexibility that characterizes the working universe in the United States—is the cause for the creation of a quantity of jobs that is still unattainable in Europe, because of the social protections inherited from the Fordist era. In the United States we therefore have a higher rate of employment but also, at the same time, a higher poverty rate than in Europe and Japan, where social protection seems to insure less poverty but at the price of very high unemployment.[31]

It is certain that in the United States, the flexibility inherent to an unregulated job market is the cause of the qualitative deterioration of the work force and of its low degree of social participation. These are the consequences of the pauperization of large sectors of the active population. Therefore, while it is true what the "Clintonian" economists Robert Reich and Paul Romer say, that in the long run excessive inequality causes negative externalities, like low educational levels and demotivation, which are ultimately harmful to economic growth, it is also true that the example of European-style social protections are no longer a realistic model for an improvement of the American work force. And in fact, it is Europe that is adopting the American "model." Most of all, comparative studies show that a politic aimed at enhancing productivity, job creation and income distribution no longer has any model from which to draw inspiration. The answer to the need of creating jobs and reducing income disparities will be (if indeed it *will* be at all) the result of a move on the part of Europe and Japan in the direction of the current American system (with more flexibility and less social protections and the negative externalities that accompany them), and a move toward a more European direction on the part of the Americans, at least for certain sectors of social protections (health care, more active social policies). Anyhow, the general trend is still one of deregulation and suppression of previously conquered social rights. If Americans are indeed drawing inspiration from the European social state, certainly they are doing it to reap its advantages, in particular the ones deriving from public education and professional training. But these advantages will materialize if, *and only if,* the European countries will not get stuck with the problems of the American system. History, and not only comparative economics, teaches us this lesson. The international monetary system, currently regulated by American policies, will surely be more than happy to supervise this unequal exchange between occupational models currently lacking in both efficiency and efficacy.

The trend towards neo-servile work relations is implicit in the new post-Fordist mode of production, and finds its origin in *the wage form* that accompanies this transformation. On the one hand, salaries are increasingly seen as an adjustable variable dependent on economic policies, in the sense that the absorption of macroeconomic shocks and market oscillations is left to the salaried employees and to them alone. On the other hand, consistent with this political choice and different from the Fordist era, the new wage rules are determined precisely in order to manage instabilities.

This is why the amount of salaried income is not specified in advance, and everything is conditional, provisional up to the very end of the company's accounting processes. To reach this goal, salaries are strongly individualized: the worker's qualifications (age, competency and initial training) determine only a part of the salary, while an increasingly important part is determined in the workplace on the basis of the worker's level of implication, of his or her "zeal" and interest as demonstrated *during* the working process and therefore *after* the negotiation phase. This is how the salary is disconnected from the position, loses its specialized connotations and gradually becomes an individual compensation.

The same position, then, can see a vast array of merit-based remunerations, since the company does not feel the obligation to apply a conventional salary grid that would be decided on a collective contractual agreement. The company, on the contrary, can elaborate another sort of salary grid, creating different levels for the same position.

We have in fact a double movement in salary dynamics: the annual salary increase (base salary) and the increase based on merit on the basis of the degree of individual or "team" implication and effort. The first increase rewards the acquired competency of the worker (the qualities that he or she possesses independently from actual performance and that are calculated contractually) and as such they are *irreversible*; the second increase rewards individual performance (or sometimes "team" performance), and as such is a *reversible* element in wage remuneration.

The servile connotation of post-Fordist work is perfectly coherent with this kind of wage relation, and specifically for that reversible and variable part of the salary that depends from the personal implication and interest in the company's fortunes on the part of the individual worker. Being variable and reversible, this remuneration based on the implication and participation of the work force is, in fact, a sort of "dividend," that is a portion of the profits realized by the company and it is tied to the final outcomes of the enterprise itself. This is why, instead of talking about salary (which is "money as capital," like they used to say in classical economic theory), one should talk about *income* (which is "money as money"). This is, in other words, a compensation for *services* rendered. It is precisely the co-presence, within the post-Fordist societies, of salary and income in the productive process that make it impossible to distinguish between industrial and service employment. To be more precise, industry has become closer to the service sector while the service sector has become industrialized because of its adoption of industrial productive techniques.

It is interesting to remark that the trend towards a servile way of regulating wage relations is in full contradiction with the official (neoclassical) theories of the job market, according to which the work force has a price (salary) determined by offer and demand, and therefore directly on the market itself, before the actual work has even started, like for any other kind of traded merchandise. Economists like George Akerlof[32]—on the wave of the research about the organizational formulas tying the workers to their company that had been initiated in 1946 by Ruth Benedict in her book about Japan[33]—have underscored how the exchange between capital and labor is an extra-mercantile one, where the dimension of "reciprocal gift" prevails, a gift of implication, interest, participation and devotion that, according to this approach, would reveal the need for belonging inherent to the individual's operation in a working group or a company. This belonging would insure that the workers receive, thanks to their enthusiasm and participation, a higher compensation than the salary determined by competition mechanisms (*ex ante*) in the job market. As Akerlof said in an interview, "In my 'gift exchange' model, unemployment develops because workers care about their coworkers. This limits the firm's ability to impose efficient contracts which would be market-clearing (with market-clearing contracts there is no unemployment)."[34]

These interpretive models of the exchange between capital and labor signal the return of the social in the explanation of economic phenomena, in particular concerning the importance of social ties for the good functioning of a company's organization. It is from this point of view that wage rules, as a confirmation of Durkheim's theories, have a social origin, because they are the expression of a "sedimentation of collective values" destined to last until it will be modified by a new contestation cycle.[35]

Unfortunately, as it was indicated by Jacques Godbout in his study on "the spirit of the gift,"[36] the introduction of the gift within the exchange between capital and labor in the explanation of the new rules from wage determination suffers from a fundamental contradiction. If it is true, as Rockefeller used to say, that "[t]he ability to deal with people is as purchasable a commodity as sugar or coffee. And I will pay more for that ability than for any other under the sun,"[37] it is also true that this "good," this "good" made of good will, loyalty, team spirit, cannot be considered a merchandise, because if not we would have started producing it a long time ago! The instrumental use of social relations is not easy to theorize, one always ends up considering human relations as a mean, as a merchandise, thereby contradicting any initial good intention (especially when the workers, after having "given themselves" to the company, receive a pink slip at the next economic crisis).

The servile dimension that imbues the post-Fordist mode of production cannot be reduced to the monetary exchange between capital and labor, nor does it derive from the "dual" society described by André Gorz, Peter Glotz, Guy Aznar and others during the 1980s. Theories of "dual society" see a decreasing number of "guaranteed" productive workers surrounded by an increasing number of "non-guaranteed" temporary workers. These theories of a two-speed society had the merit of underscoring the trend toward the increase in servile work behind phenomena of pauperization, unemployment and temporary employment. They are wrong, however, in distinguishing between a core of wealth-producing workers and another constituted of consumers, on the basis of a "servant-master" relationship. They don't understand that this distinction traverses the entirety of the working world: there is the same servility in the relation between the housekeeper and the people who pay her just as in the one between the producer of industrial goods and his or her employer.[38]

The "two societies" are in fact indistinguishable from the point of view of wealth production, even if the economic mechanism (the parceling and differentiating of the work force according to income levels), does create a hierarchy of workers. But both in the first and the second society we find the same human essence, whether one produces or not, whether one works in a factory or at home, in a hospital or a bank. We cannot get rid of the highest level of industrialism with a more just distribution of his organizational forms, lulled by the belief that this would allow us to reconstitute an autonomous domestic (private) sphere free from the relations based on command and discipline characteristic of the wage-based labor (public) sphere.

We will soon come back to this issue. For now, we can just remember that the distinction between "productive" and "unproductive" work found in classical economics from Adam Smith to Karl Marx always had a political—even more than economical—value. For the classics it was crucial to establish the centrality of the Industrial Worker at a time when reactionary forces wanted to stop development, and to stop the transformation of the economy from the agricultural to the industrial stage. From a theoretical point of view, it is very clear that there is an uncertainty in the classics' treatment of the so-called "unproductive workers," although it is often masked by dismissive judgments about the reactionary function of the mass of agricultural serfs. Marx himself, who had put all his bets on the industrial workers, will end up affirming, in his comment on Mandeville's *Fable of the Bees*, that thieves, rogues and striking workers are also productive, since thieves, for instance, inspired the invention of locks, jurisprudence, manuals and academic tenure, while striking workers forced capital to invest in new machineries aimed at eliminating conflicts ("machines go where workers strike": Marx said long before Galbraith did).[39]

Paradoxically, those who persist in distinguishing between productive workers and serfs on the basis of doubtful economic theories (to the point that Schumpeter considered the controversy about this issue a complete waste of time), while they have the noble intention of redistributing work equally between the employed and the unemployed, they end up proposing *conservative* models for political action. In fact, in the last two decades, it is precisely within the reproductive world—the universe of women— that *new political subjectivities, rationalities and forms of struggle* have been born. There is a desire to shrink the service sector in parallel with the decline of "productive" industrial labor, in order to allow everybody to work while simultaneously reconstructing the private sphere and the tasks currently performed by "neo-servile" workers. But in so doing, we run the risk of forgetting the only political subjectivities that have emerged during these years marked by economic transformation and the extension/generalization of industrial relations to the social sphere. Today, our most pressing problem is not a more equitable distribution of labor, but of *income*: it is on this basis that we can define the *meaning* that we want to attribute to different *activities*. Only later will we justify their retribution, independently from their productive or reproductive nature.

The real problem is the elaboration of political practices able to overturn the latent servility to be found across all working activities through instances of social recomposition and *political community*. Even if today segmentation and discrimination prevail within the universe of work and reproduction (even between the salaried woman and her housekeeper), this does not mean that we need to back and impose a distribution of labor without taking into consideration the different subjectivities unwittingly produced by the "industrialization" of society.

The servile dimension of post-Fordist work originates precisely from the linguistic-communicative mediation innervating the *entire* economic process. On the one hand we appeal to what is common to all human beings, that is, the ability of communicating, while on the other hand this shared universal (public) ability leads to increasingly personalized, privatized and therefore servile hierarchies in the working environment. On the one hand we want to *co*-operate, and communicative work allows us to do that, but on the other we also want to re-*divide*, create hierarchies, segment and privatize the public—because common to all—resource of communicative action.

Today's working assignments increasingly take place in the field of "relations" between people. Professionalism is less defined in "industrial" terms, and more as "services to the individual." This last aspect is ever more essential to the functioning of the economic process.

The importance of relational work is proven, among other things, by the crisis that the notion of "total quality," typical of post-Fordist Toyotism, is already traversing, notwithstanding all the efforts made to perfect it during the last decade with the help of more sophisticated organizational techniques.

We now understand that the *total quality management*,[40] with its organizational techniques, its models of flexible handling of the work force, its quality circles and so on, is *no longer sufficient*. The crisis resides in the excessive insistence on product quality standards, without giving enough consideration to *the aims* of production which, in a market economy, is only related to *the sale* of goods and services. There is one example, recently used to reflect on the crisis of the "lean production" models, which deserves to be cited.[41]

In the 1980s, the United Parcel Service (UPS), an American company that specializes in express mail and package delivery, had concentrated all its energy on providing an extremely fast service to its customers. "To better serve the client," UPS had reduced the time given to its drivers to a minimum, squeezing them to the last second and increasing their hourly productivity. As a consequence, the number of workers devoted to the distribution of parcels had decreased.

But to its great surprise, UPS discovered that its clients cared about the timely delivery of their orders only up to a certain point, while they were much more interested in having a longer "interaction" with the drivers—who where their only *face-to-face* point of contact with UPS. If the drivers had been less efficient and had more time to chat with the customers, the latter would have been able to acquire more knowledge about the different services offered by UPS.

This is when the "service to the person," the direct relation with the client, clearly recognized as essential to the expansion of the company's business, led UPS to increase the time devoted to the communication between drivers and customers, thereby creating the real conditions for the hiring of new workers and to increase their salaries in the form of bonuses.

Post-Fordist "total quality" does not stop the production of goods and services, but includes the sphere of distribution, sales consumption, and reproduction. This is why communicative-relational work, which normally is defined as activities of care or of general services to the person, acquires a universal value. In post-Fordism, work has taken on a servile connotation *because* communicative-relational action, although increasingly relevant in economic terms, is not correctly recognized. Thus, work becomes an opportunity to impose personal hierarchies where one worker has authority over the other, and becomes the terrain where attitudes, feelings and dispositions such as cynicism, fear or denunciation can grow and fester. But the servile connotation of work is not founded on the distinction between productive and nonproductive work, but on the absence of economic compensation for communicative-relational activities.

8. The New Economic Cycle

The "measure," or rather, the indicator of the structural changes that we have described, is given by the dynamics peculiar to the new economic cycle of the early 1990s. Undoubtedly, the most surprising characteristic of the new post-Fordist cycle is the slow and noninflationary nature of its expansive phases. A slow growth with modest inflationary rates contradicts the traditional dynamics of the economic cycle, where inflation should follow the attaining of a "natural rate" of unemployment and the full utilization of productive capacities. In classical dynamics of the economic cycle, when unemployment goes below a certain level, businesses agree to increase their wages in order to recruit employees and transfer the cost on prices. At the same time, they also increase prices as a response to a demand surpassing the current offer (which indicates the maximum use of productive capacity).[42]

However, the post-Fordist economic cycle contradicts this theory, preventing the economic indicators from performing their function and thereby displacing the monetary authorities who, on the basis of these same indicators, decide to prevent inflation intervening on monetary instruments.[43] There are several reasons for this phenomenon.

First of all, the very nature of the post-Fordist regime of growth implies a push towards a maximum of market expansion (which implies increased deregulation, and the suppression of all protectionist norms aimed at defending local markets). This brings to the globalization of corporate functioning, in the pursuit not only of lower labor costs, but also of strategic positions on foreign markets in order to fully exploit any sale potential. Globalization is a consequence of the reversal in the relation between production and market which led to the post-Fordist restructuration of production processes. Market saturation can't but create the conditions for a ferocious competition between same-sector companies on the same markets. Rather than increase prices, even when demand is growing, producers prefer to realize their profits saving on labor costs.

Corporate globalization allows responding to the variations in demand internal to each country with a *global offer*. If plant capacity is maxed out in the United States, Mexican, Chinese or European factories—which often are still American-owned—can provide the offer instead and thereby satisfy the demand in the United States. In other words, in a global economy the notion of "national productive capacity" no longer has any operational meaning.

Secondly, the risk of a cost-based inflation caused by salary increases as a consequence of the decrease in unemployment numbers is significantly lowered in the post-Fordist expansion cycle. In recessionary phases, on the contrary, the net loss of jobs, the increase in temporary work and the fear of unemployment (a fear that increases as the guarantees provided by the Social State and union representation progressively fade away) create a population with "lower expectations," according to the economist Paul Krugman, currently teaching at MIT.[44]

The social conflicts in the post-Fordist cycle also reveal very important changes in the tactics of the parties involved: on the one hand, trade unions are often forced to accept salary or benefit reductions in order to insure that their members' jobs won't be eliminated; on the other hand, when resistance to management pressure is stronger, the employers resort to outsourcing to companies who pay less, and employees are not unionized and are hired *just-in-time*.

The example of the three-week strike by the 75,000 unionized America teamsters in April 1994 is often cited precisely in order to illustrate the change in power relations that has occurred in the post-Fordist economic cycle. The same strike lasted only ten days in 1989 and had paralyzed the American economy, whereas five years later that same economy continued its uninterrupted expansion.

The transportation sector, given its strategic role in a *just-in-time* economy based on the spatial circulation of raw materials, parts and completed products, is the one that best exemplifies the logic of deregulation policies: networked corporations; systematic recourse to subcontracting to reduce costs and increase productivity; de-professionalization of direct labor, especially in maintenance positions, often with disastrous consequences for the environment and the safety of passengers whose safety is subordinated to the one of merchandise; maximum plant exploitation in order to accelerate the amortization of fixed capital expenditures; and increased reliance on temporary workers. In the recessive phase of the cycle we observe an acceleration of restructuring processes in the sense of deregulation, which effectively deprives the work force of a classical instrument of resistance against salary compression and professional devaluation such as the strike.[45]

Therefore, it is not on the salary front that inflation can take on again. The weakening of the workers' contractual power and the spatial re-articulation of production act in such a way that salaries always increase less than productivity, which causes the unitary decrease of labor costs. The real decrease in salary income also causes (and this is new) consumer pressure toward an increased quality of services and a slowing down in prices, as is happening today in the American health sector. Resistance on the consumer services front exists as a reaction to the weakening in power relations on the income creation and distribution front, and brings about restructuring and rationalization processes in the service sector as well, on the wave of the post-Fordist techniques already used in the industrial sector. In the service sector, then, traditionally a source of inflation because of its scarce productivity, we cannot expect a push toward an inflationist increase in prices.

Post-Fordist technologies, because of their informational-communicative nature, bring about decisive effects on all sectors of production, accelerating the increase in productivity of the entire economic system. Classic indicators can't measure the productivity increases induced, for instance, by the use of optical scanners in supermarket cash registers (reduction in the rotation times of consumer goods), or by the power increase of computers and video-communicative technologies. These indicators were determined in a material economy, and can't deliver statistical data on the *information flows* that are the basis of today's immaterial economy.[46]

A definition of productivity in terms of output per hour worked does not, apparently, allow us to expect spectacular increases in productivity in the next few years. However, such a definition does not take into account the productive potential inherent to information technologies and the new corporate models of organization. Productive potential, in fact, is no longer measurable purely on the basis of the relation between investment expenses and prices: we know very well that corporations are massively investing in high-technology goods whose prices are always decreasing. This, however, does not mean that we can underestimate the increase in investments, thinking that if the prices decrease, the volume of investments does not seem that impressive in "real" terms. In fact, the new technologies are much more than "better typewriters"! The benefits of this new wave of investments will not materialize immediately, since the restructuring of working practices and of professional training will take some time, but it is on *this* terrain that the stakes of the innovations in production are played out, and not at all on the quantitative relation between invested capitals and sale prices.

The globalization of the economy, the investments in restructuring, the mutation of social conflicts and the improvements in the service sector are all part of the post-Fordist cycle which, in their interaction, prevent inflation from rising during expansion periods. On the other hand, the centrality of communicative interaction and of immaterial forms of organization within the productive processes decreases the risks of inflation deriving from possible increases in the cost of raw materials such as oil. In a post-materialist era, the most important raw materials are the knowledge, the intelligence, and the other cognitive-immaterial qualities activated during the productive process. When it comes to determining the final price of goods and services, the physical raw materials, which were fundamental during the Fordist era, are now less important than immaterial human resources.

This does not mean that the real nature of the post-Fordist economic cycle would, all by itself, lead the monetary authorities to eschew raising interest rates when prices start to increase. The opposite is actually true: monetary authorities, fearing a highly unlikely inflation, in fact risk creating it themselves, destabilizing the financial and monetary markets and creating self-fulfilling expectations.

Monetary authorities, of course, do their job, which consists in preventing inflationary spirals acting on monetary instruments. What seems almost certain by now is that their indicators are inadequate to articulate an effective response to the dynamics of the post-Fordist cycle. It is in fact on the basis of the tension between "real" and "monetary" economy that economic cycles are now synchronized. The United States, Europe and Japan—three "poles" whose economic cycles were not synchronized in the past (to the great advantage of the United States)—are now headed toward a progressive synchronization of their respective cycles.

In fact, while it is true that in the global post-Fordist economy we have a global offer of goods and services, it is true that the demand has also become irreversibly global. The deregulation of financial markets at the beginning of the 1990s leads to the synchronization of economic cycles because, thanks to the international mobility of capitals, it accelerates post-Fordist reconstruction where it is still lagging while retarding economic expansion where the reconstruction of productive processes has already occurred. As a consequence, in the global economy the currency of the country closest to the end of the expansion phase is devalued with respect to the ones of still recovering countries.

This is what happened in 1994. Paradoxically, the rise in interest rates in the United States decided by the Federal Reserve in order to anticipate an inflationary recovery, were accompanied by a devaluation of the dollar. This contradicted all those who still thought that higher interest rates would attract European and Japanese capital and strengthen the dollar. The opposite happened: the dollar was devalued, allowing the American economy to increase its exports (and profits) in a period when the American commercial balance was deteriorating (because of the strong growth in internal demand in the recovery of 1993–1994 while foreign demand was stagnating in countries that were still restructuring themselves). The strengthening of other currencies, on the other hand, put the brakes on the rise of interest rates in still recovering countries. Thus, Europe and Japan did not need to smolder their recovery, or to reduce their imports from the United States. Without a modification of exchange rates as the result of the "strange" devaluation of the dollar, European and Japanese interest rates would have increased much more rapidly.

The United States, Europe and Japan are now synchronizing their economic cycles as follows: the American expansive phase extends itself thanks to the devaluation of the dollar, thus insuring an increase in the global demand for goods and services, and it will stop as soon as the European and Japanese economies will be forced to decelerate their recovery as a consequence of an excessive increase in their interest rates. In 1994, the European economies were buttressed by exports to North America, Latin America and the Eastern European countries, while the internal demand for durable goods didn't give any real sign of recovery. This kept inflation low and, symmetrically, interest rates high.

We can say, then, that the crisis of economic indicators contributes to accelerating globalization, not only in the productive processes (that is, the creation of the offer), but also in the demand for goods and services. On the one hand, in a strongly liberalized international financial market we can only talk about a *global offer for money*, and on the other the noninflationary nature of post-Fordist economic recoveries moves capital according to a new and different rationality. Capital moves from one market to the next, anticipating *just-in-time* the variations in demand, *independently* from the variations in real interest rates. In fact, it could not be otherwise in an economic regime characterized by an abundance of capital availability dominated by oscillations in demand on which one needs to capitalize. If this is the case, as seems plausible given the dynamic of the economic cycles during the first half of the 1990s, the contradictory relation between interest rates and currency valuations are in fact perfectly coherent within the Fordist paradigm.

As further proof, we can look at the increasing globalization in American investments. Between 1992 and 1994, American investments abroad have vastly expanded. As the economic recovery in the rest of the world started to consolidate, capital shifted outside of the United States. The very slow increase in the prices of goods and services and the prudent policies of the central banks, aimed at moderating the global offer of money, caused American investors to believe that the recovery in Europe, Japan and the developing countries was immune from exaggerated inflationary risks. *The global investor*, then, will not see the value of financial investments abroad decrease in the near future.[47] In fact, in real terms, Japanese and German interest rates are higher than the American ones, precisely because inflation, in these countries, was close to zero. Furthermore, the growth in internal demand within the United States has been possible, until now, thanks to a record reduction in domestic savings (3.8 percent of available income) during the year 1994, and a parallel increase in consumer credit.

This is how we can explain the apparent paradox of dollar devaluation combined with repeated increases in American interest rates: capital has gone where the investors anticipated an increase in demand (lower inflation rates and higher savings available for spending with respect to the United States). The heterodox saying according to which it is demand that drives the offer has never been more pertinent than in post-Fordism.

The fact remains that developed countries, and the United States in particular, are playing a decisive game with respect to inflation. On the one hand there are those who believe that an "inflationary spiral" is around the corner, even if at the end of 1994 there is still no sign of this happening. The inflationary hawks do all they can to force monetary authorities to increase interest rates, trying to protect the income (the rents) of Treasury bonds investors. And in fact, the only winner in this kind of policy is the highest income bracket, which detains the majority of bonds. The middle and lower income bracket, on the contrary, are the ones most in debt, and in this conjuncture they suffer from a further reduction in their available income. This situation results in a worsening of the discrepancies in income distribution. On the other hand, noninflationary economic growth, because of its characteristics, cannot be managed by a manipulation of interest rates, and this ends up favoring those who want to regulate economic cycles with fiscal policies. *Real* interest rates, which are the result of the difference between nominal rates and the rate of inflation, are already very high, to the point that private banks are vastly expanding their credit offer, making the policies of the central banks even less effective.[48] All of this just confirms that a redefinition of statistical indicators on the basis of the post-Fordist economic transformation is extremely urgent.

In the last analysis, the synchronization of the economic cycles radically modifies the rationality of international wealth distribution. The American, European and Japanese growth engines are establishing new hierarchies among themselves and with the rest of the world. These hierarchies are not determined solely by their economic strength, but, increasingly, as a result of their respective position within the global information flow. In this respect, the fact that in the Chinese province of Huang Dong the growth rate is 15 percent while in the United States it only amounts to 2 or 3 percent is not that important.[49] What counts much more is the fact that the global system of telecommunication networks is growing to a *monthly* rate of 15 percent, because this is the rate measuring a growth in *power* and the global hierarchies that it creates from the "command" exerted on these new strategic resources. It is the command exerted on the globalization of information-communicative networks that will decide the new international division of power. Power is rapidly proceeding to the creation of hierarchies in the international access to the property of knowledge, whose costs are increasingly decisive in the determination of the relative prices of internationally traded goods and services. From now on, patents, copyrights, trademarks and trade secrets will be the real stake of all international treaties.[50]

The redefinition of the international division of political and economical command is not the fruit of chance, but instead follows the geographical lines traced by investments in the telecommunication networks. The times for profit-taking are defined by the resistance to the barriers to foreign capital penetration raised by different countries, that is, to their status with respect to deregulation. The position of each country will depend on its ability to capitalize on immaterial labor and knowledge, and on the possibility of transfering the costs of knowledge on relative prices, which are the true bearers of the "unequal exchanges" existing between the new centers and the new peripheries, between the new North and the new South.

In this kind of economic geopolitics, "Europe does not fail because it declines, but because it fails to accept this decline, because it resists it rather than insisting on it."[51] But insisting on the decline of this Europe, a "mausoleum of memories," a place of merciless competition among member countries, violence and fratricidal struggles, means building a European union founded on the collective knowledge that the continent will be able to produce.

In the post-Fordist economy, where immaterial labor acquires a strategic value, only the European state can be extraterritorial, that is, a state that values local knowledge and does not kill it with the imposition of rules, norms and exchange rates inherited from the Fordist regime of growth and the international exchange system that characterized it. This only reproduces on the European scale the "dual society" that we have already mentioned.[52] The free circulation of merchandise is left impotent if it does not become a "free circulation of knowledge" and a free circulation of the social identities that it produces. In order to be "free," local knowledge has to be recognized through an international mechanism of redistribution that would guarantee the continuity of local and regional investments in Research and Development. Without taking this step, the European Union is not "destined to decline," but has already done so.

The analysis of the post-Fordist economic cycle, with its "strangeness" in respect to previous ones, has revealed not only the nature of this innovative and restructuring leap but also the urgent necessity to elaborate new rules in order to confront the dangers that we are currently facing.

2

Rules for the Incommensurable

1. The Fair of Meanings

In the years between the second half of the 1970s and the explosion of the recession of 1989–1991 (United States) and 1991–1994 (Europe and Japan), the gradual emergence of post-Fordism generated a growing "existential malaise," a climate of pervasive insecurity, a social and political disorientation whose explanation exceeds the conjunctural data.[1] This climate of uncertainty, the *"no future"* widely anticipated by some youth movements of the 1970s, can be attributed to several factors: mass unemployment; the pauperization and occupational instability of ever increasing sectors of the population; the awareness that investments were creating less occupation and that in absolute numbers they were in fact reducing it; problems related to the aging of the population and the financial difficulties these problems were beginning to cause. But it is only in the years of the recession that what had previously remained latent emerged in its full gravity and complexity. The recession of the early 1990s simply tore away the "veil of ignorance" which allowed us to postpone addressing the new socioeconomic paradigm politically.

Before analyzing the roots of this "crisis of meaning" and its most immediate political implications, we need to consider the reasons for the time lag between the processes of social transformation, the emerging awareness of the mechanisms behind these processes, and the crisis of the political forms intended to govern the transformation.

First we should ask ourselves: What are the times of diffusion proper to a new productive paradigm such as today's new "universal instrument," the computer (or "language machine")? Today the computer corresponds to what the electrical motor was a century ago, and the steam engine before then.

In response to a question about the times of diffusion proper to the new information technologies, Andrew S. Grove, founder and CEO of the Intel Corporation, explained in an interview to *Business Week* that the experience of innovation is different from that of immigration. A Hungarian immigrant who escaped from his country during the 1956 revolution, Grove arrived in the United States at the beginning of the 1960s. He went on to become one of the famous Silicon Valley pioneers. According to him, the difference between innovation and immigration resides in the fact that immigration is a break, a radical separation between a before and an after, while technological transformation is an experience that is lived minute by minute in everyday life. The latter transition is gradual: at a certain point we find ourselves holding in our hands an electrical razor or an automatic toothbrush. We actually make the experience of the new "universal machine" when it has *already* become part of our everyday life, when it has already entered our homes and our children's *gadgets*.[2] Leaving one's own country, as in the biblical exodus, is a different experience because it implies laceration and suffering, and thus the awareness of what is happening in one's life. When we leave, we always think we will come back one day to embrace our friends and family, to see the colors, hear the sounds and smell the air of the country where we were born. If we can't go back, memory will do all it can to preserve what we have left behind:

> There are two types of Hungarian immigrants of my age: the people who were constantly bitching about America because they couldn't find the things they left behind in Hungary, and people who accepted what was available here as a kind of moral equivalent of what was left behind. Once you got into that mode, you went with the flow and did quite well. The others were still bitching "they don't have sidewalk cafés in New York." This is a little like that.[3]

The "universal machine" affirms itself gradually, minute by minute. When the crisis explodes, revealing to everyone the epochal nature of the transformation, it's already "too late." We can't go back; either we go with the flow or we keep resenting our time. Either we try to extract the "moral equivalent" of a previous time, or we poison our lives with resentment, appealing to ever-fading memories. The new does not erase the past, but only that which makes the past a kind of ballast, a dead weight preventing us from facing the future with intelligence and with the capacity for producing new affect and new political struggles. During this transition, the long time periods necessary for the diffusion of the new "universal machine" clash with the shortness of the average life span. As in the biblical flight from Egypt, we hurriedly take our most precious belongings so that we will be able to "wander" in the new world without getting lost. Normally, these are the things that we can hide at the border. And the thing easiest to import "clandestinely" into the new world is *friendship*, the "bridge over the abyss" that allows the wanderer to cross unknown territories—the same friendship that Deleuze and Guattari conceptualized before parting forever.[4]

On the basis of such considerations, the following remarks by Andy Grove seem less surprising:

> One of the most dramatic applications of computer technology is airline reservation systems. The reason it's so dramatic is that you bridge time and place to reserve a seat on a flight that is at a different time and a different place, while sitting at the counter. It's a communication application.[5]

What is surprising here is not only the concrete example, which is the most banal and familiar of things, especially when compared to sophisticated discourses about artificial intelligence, but also the reference to a "fourth dimension" which radically transforms even the revolutionary notion of the space-time relation introduced in the twentieth century. Subjectively, we live the daily experience of processes that are revolutionizing our way of viewing things, our categories of thought, our scientific theories, but this subjective and simple experience, which slowly shapes our perception of time and space, clashes with political languages that were created in a different era, and which are emptied of any reference to what we experience in our daily lives.

Political discourse's delayed reaction to the post-Fordist transformation can also be explained with regard to what has happened in the world of scientific research. Academic circles are becoming increasingly closed and restricted, more and more specialized and protective. More generally, the post-Fordist transformation has seen an increase in disciplinary specialization—a multiplication of research fields whose origin is to be found in the obsession of having to measure and quantify everything.

Scientific research's endemic tendency to distinguish between what can be rigorously demonstrated and what can only be discussed ends up opening a rift between two equally important aspects of the discourse on society, "allowing those who dream of the white smock of the 'scientist' to avoid discussing the themes that are most difficult and urgent in the social sphere," in the words of economist Giacomo Becattini. During the post-Fordist transformation, quantitative scientific research, particularly in the economic field, led to a *social de-responsabilization* of economists. This contributed further to the weakening of the critical autonomy of citizens, who were faced with a proliferation of *prêt-à-porter* ideologies that would have been far more pertinent in the discourse about sports ("success at all costs") than in the critique of our existence.

One could develop an analysis of the insufficiencies intrinsic to the various scientific disciplines, and in particular of the technicization of disciplinary languages. We will limit ourselves to quoting Fraser's admonition, pronounced over fifty years ago: "When the phenomena of economic life change, the meanings of the words that we use to describe them change too." We could add that scientific thought's "diaspora," its retreat from the most obvious social changes into a quantitative analysis intended to avoid the interrogation of society's general development, is symptomatic of the scientist's *fear* of losing credibility in the eyes of politicians. In many cases, this has fostered various forms of servile careerism. What is more, Nietzsche has explained very clearly how the will to power is at work in quantitative research; the latter "deprives the world of its most frightening aspects. The fear of the incalculable as the secret instinct of science."

Methodologically, the scientific research of the last two decades has adopted a "strategy of deferral." By isolating and rigidifying different disciplines and professions, research has organized itself in such a way that it can defer to other disciplines whatever threatens the internal coherence of its own field of inquiry. One deferral at a time, research has denied itself the very possibility of examining change. In fact, "change" has become the object of a research discipline, aggravating the fragmentation of knowledge by one more compartment of specialized discourse. The mechanism by which the analysis of change is delegated to psychology, sociology, or even technology (if not simply to televised debates) has emptied scientific research of every dialectical concept, without which we are unable to understand anything at all.

Some have described our current situation as a "crisis of meaning"—an incapacity to elaborate and propose to to all members of society a system of references (ideas, norms, values, ideals) that makes it possible to give to one's existence a stable and coherent meaning, to develop an identity, to communicate with others, to participate in the construction—real or imaginary—of a liveable world. This state of affairs is not a consequence of our society being characterized by a radical absence of meaning. The opposite is true: we live in a genuine "fair of meanings" where each of us can "freely" appropriate the images, symbols and myths that s/he prefers. What we lack is a "symbolic order" capable of structuring and unifying the scattered fragments of our lives.

This lack of meaning, intended as the absence of a "symbolic order," is without doubt the point at which the historical development of capital and its vocation to uproot and decode everything culminate. The economy, which has never been more global, annihilates ancient rituals and ceremonies, strips nation states of their power, and disaggregates the nuclear family. Races too are disappearing, "drowning" in processes of immaterial production where the colors and smells of every agent can be reproduced artificially. We thought capitalism would create the conditions for perfect happiness by destroying every sense of *belonging*, by the nomadism of the rootless individual that results from the "deterritorialization" intrinsic to the development of the global economy. Now we have reached the apex of globalization and capitalist "deterritorialization," and everything is returning: the Family, the nation state, religious fundamentalism. Everything is returning—but in a perverted, reactionary, conservative way, as the philosopher predicted. At the very time when the "absence of meaning" brings within our reach an era in which human beings finally seem able to speak to one another, by virtue of free access to communication, we are witnessing the return of the idea of "race" and of every myth of origin and belonging. The potential liberty of the "transparent society" turns into its opposite: a racist intolerance that defends the borders of its homeland. The only thing that matters is the myth, the symbol, the semblance of a historical origin capable of dominating chaos with hatred.

At this point, the suspicion arises that those who present the quest for a new "symbolic order," a new "social model," or a "new utopia" as a humanist denunciation of the emptiness brought about by capitalist development are actually constructing their argument on the wrong premises. It's not a matter of contesting the noble spirit of those searching for alternatives to the chaos overwhelming us, but rather of avoiding a situation in which illusions are nourished with further illusions, in which the constant "need for meaning" is met with formulas more likely to aggravate our condition than to improve it.

Before defining the rules needed to prevent the current deregulation from leading into generalized war, it is necessary, therefore, to think about the "places" where rules are born and constructed. In what follows, this will be done by analyzing the "rule" implicit in the (constitutional) principle of the equality of the sexes.

2. The Place for the Socks

The debate over domestic labor, or over the reproductive labor "historically" performed by women, furnishes insights essential to the search for rules and for the *measuring unit* that defines these rules. These insights are necessary for confronting the deregulation that rages unchecked in the age of post-Fordism.

There is a controversy between those who consider domestic work economically productive and demand its remuneration ("wages for housework") and those who define domestic labor as a form of "labor for oneself" indispensable for the preservation of the private sphere. Those who take the second view demand a generalized reduction of wage labor ("work less so all can work") and a cooperative approach to housework involving men and women alike. The controversy between these two positions is only apparently "old." It is in fact highly relevant to our time.

The critics of the wages for housework model contend that this proposal involves the risk of excluding women from the economic sphere while perpetuating the obligation of men to work full-time. These critics (such as André Gorz) also hold that if we really want to consider the family an autonomous and indivisible unit, we need to establish a perfect *reciprocity* between male and female domestic activities. "Personal services" would then have to be withdrawn from the logic of wage labor and transformed into an opportunity for reclaiming "ownership of ourselves" (or control over the private sphere). This would involve overcoming the sexual division of labor typical of capitalism (a division that implies the double burden of waged and domestic labor for women).

Those are the terms of the theoretical and political debate. It would seem that this way of considering the issue misses several key points. As it happens, domestic and reproductive work has taken the form of wage labor for quite some time, at least tendentially—but it has done so in a way that reproduces class division and exploitation *between* women.

During the past decades, many reproductive activities formerly performed within the family have become services available on the market: food preparation; laundry work; house cleaning; care for children, elderly people, the disabled, and the ill. The market for services that involve caring for people, a very intensive kind of labor, has expanded, creating the need for an army of female workers that is increasingly composed of women belonging to "ethnic minorities" or to immigrant groups whose members are "prepared" to accept lower pay. The "salarization" of domestic labor—labor performed by "household aids" within the household and by service workers outside it—has altered neither the sexual nor the racial division of labor, but it has created a hierarchy within domestic labor itself. On one side of the division, one finds middle-class women (mainly white); on the other, one finds women who often belong to other ethnic groups and who have little bargaining power.

This development seems to confirm Gorz's hypothesis, according to which we need to reduce the sphere of waged repro-ductive work ("neo-servile" and poorly paid personal services) in order to reestablish equality not just between men and women but also among women.

But to stop here is to leave the argument incomplete, analyti-cally insufficient and, most of all, politically weak. Ethnological studies have shown how difficult it is to achieve a sexual equality defined in purely juridical terms, without consideration of the real, subjective dynamics at play within the fabric of conjugal life and relations of partnership.

Jean-Claude Kauffmann, a French sociologist specializing in the study of family and everyday life, writes that "the core of the resistance to gender equality is to be found in the family, in the home, in the most elementary domestic practices."[6] Detailed analysis of domestic work reveals that there is a difference in the *intensity* of the work performed by men and women even when labor time and the level of technological development are the same. According to Taylor's theory of "scientific management," an intensification of labor has occurred when a greater quantity of goods is produced in the same time, with the same technology, and by the same number of male and female workers. The increased productivity results from an acceleration of the rhythm of work, achieved by the elimination of the workday's "pores" (that is, of "dead" production time).

Countless examples could be invoked to illustrate this concept. One is that of the pair of socks. For a man, the socks are in their proper place when a woman doesn't think so at all. She ends up putting them in the place that she considers to be the right one. In bypassing the verbal stage and simply putting the socks back "where they belong," the woman creates a new habit that modifies the initial positions of the two partners. She reproduces and aggravates sexual division. Field research shows that, when their partner is away, only 65 percent of men take care of their laundry, compared to 90 percent of women. Similarly, only 44 percent of men iron their clothes, compared to 87 percent of women. The reason lies in the specific function played by clothing in the relationship between the sexes: clothing is a pivotal "tool" in feminine seduction.

Technology, represented by the washing machine (constant capital), is certainly helping men to appropriate some domestic activities, but men still refuse to establish an excessively intimate relationship with their laundry, and don't respect it very much. Men have invented washing machines, but clearly this invention has not been sufficient for developing a relation of quantitative reciprocity between men and women.

The notion that women have of the "proper place for the socks" has a long history. An infinity of sexual and social classifications are preserved in the housewife's simple gesture. The accumulation of countless silent gestures traversing the entire gamut of domestic labor forces us to speak with great caution of sexual reciprocity and the reconstruction of the private sphere through the equitable distribution of housework. *Even within* a juridical and economic framework premised on sexual equality, the exploitation of women by men is reproduced.

The issue has political implications beyond the strictly domestic sphere—implications concerning the question of measure. No jurist and no economist will ever be able to adequately define the measuring unit by which to equitably quantify male-female parity, except in an *a posteriori* manner. Even with equal rights and working schedules, different histories and sensibilities recreate hierarchies and forms even when their juridical *form* is considered to have been overcome.

The "place for the socks," the silent gesture that condenses thousands of years of sexual role distribution, poses the question of rights on a *qualitatively* new level. Amartya Sen is right to point out that, in conventional economic theory, "individuals and firms are visible," but families are not, such that the attempt to elaborate an economic theory of the family merely results in the application of market models to exchanges between family members: "Conceptualizing marriage as a 'two-person firm with either member being the entrepreneur who hires the other and receives residual profits' can perhaps be said to be a rather simple view of a very complex relationship."[7]

It's not a matter of questioning the *need* for a measuring device capable of defining as equitably as possible the exchanges that take place between men and women *within* the family unit. Years of research into the "new forms of poverty" have allowed for the development of "equivalency scales" that allow for improvements in the distribution of wealth between domestic economies, but little attention has been paid to redistribution within the family unit (with one exception: the case of single-parent households, in which the child is treated like a husband).

What needs to be discussed is the *nature* of the measuring device. The economic measuring device, which reproduces the juridical principle of sexual equality within the family sphere, reveals a *break* in the very possibility of comparing the work performed by men and women. Family life certainly involves elements of cooperation and conflict—elements that define the "problem of negotiation" between members of the family unit. But the exchange between male and female labor cannot be reduced to its "unionized" dimension, which is legally regulated by lawyers in the courtroom (as in the cases of alimony payments or divorce). Male-female exchange transcends its "unionized" form. It transcends the quantitative dimension of negotiations concerned only with "precise economic value." This is true even in the best of cases, when the assessment of women's domestic activities involves an extension of the concept of family *patrimony*, such that the income capacities of the husband are recognized as dependent on the wife's willingness to perform a series of supporting duties.[8]

The *idea* of sexual equality is strongly developed on the level of society and on that of contract negotiation, but not on the individual level. Inequality insinuates itself in the rift between representation (universality of the law) and real practices (concrete singularity of habits)—between the *formal* and the *material* constitution. Much like that of sexual harassment, the question of housework involves issues of power and authority. This is precisely why we are confronted with *incommensurable* criteria of valuation. It is useless to pretend that we are eliminating male power simply by subordinating male-female exchange to a common regime of equality. No such regime exists, because the exchange will always involve a *supplement* and a subjective *difference*—a disparity in experience that escapes any reduction to units of measure, units applied to qualitatively heterogeneous quantities of concrete labor.

As is well known, the problem of measure can be approached on various levels. First of all, there is the need to abstract from the variety of concrete tasks performed: there are those who iron clothes and those who take care of the children, those who work outside and those who work within the home. In the case of domestic work, the process of abstraction is usually effected by comparing the different activities in terms of labor time (where a specialist job requires a certain amount of training time, this time is included in the calculation). However, and as was seen in the example of the "proper place" for the socks, this abstraction is violently thwarted by the "lived history" of women, which problematizes the reduction to temporal units and the attempt to measure the work performed. Even if the hours worked are the same, the tasks performed by women are much more intensive than those of men. This intensity cannot be reduced to a purely quantitative dimension, as if it were the straightforward result of a specialist knowledge acquired over time (from childhood onward); rather, it reflects the division of sexual roles. Behind the disparity in labor intensity lies an entire history of *asymmetrical* power relationships. The *power* exercised over women sends into crisis the very possibility of measuring quantities of labor time while applying the same unit of measure to both sexes.

In the light of a careful analysis of domestic work processes, the definition of the parity of rights on the basis of reciprocity, or of the equal distribution of working time between men and women, reveals its profound political inadequacy. The quantity of hours worked may be the same, it may even include the training time necessary for specializing in certain functions, but we conflate in the same unit of measurement subjective and historical experiences that are in fact completely heterogeneous. Within the One, the measuring unit, difference hides (in this case the difference between men and women) and multiplicities dwell.

It has to be clear that what we have said regarding male-female exchange in the private sphere has a *general* significance; it concerns the very core of the paradigm guiding the transformation of the capitalist mode of production. The first to realize that there is a contradiction inherent to the exchange of equivalent quantities of labor time (the exchange on the basis of which wages are determined on the labor market) was none other than Adam Smith, the father of political economy. Smith pointed out that the quantity of work *contained* in the commodities purchased by the worker with his contractually determined wages is one thing, the quantity of work *commanded* during the labor process another. The wage commands more labor than is necessary for the reproduction of the commodities corresponding to the wage. Command is exerted over labor once the worker enters the production process; the worker's activity is completely determined by the machines and the organization of the plant, which belong to the capitalist. It is precisely because of this crisis in measurement, very lucidly indicated by Smith, that economic growth and development occur. In fact, if the salary commands more work than is contained in the commodities corresponding to the wage, this command measures labor productivity and, consequently, *capitalist* growth.[9]

From Smith onward, economic science has done all it could to eliminate the contradiction that lies at the origin of the incommensurable. What economic science has tried to do is eliminate the qualitative aspect, the "place for the socks," the surplus behind which is hidden the history of the subjective difference between those who work and those who give orders. In other words, economic science has tried to solve *logically* a contradiction pertaining to the political sphere of power relations, by simplifying inherently differentiated and dialectical categories in terms of formal identities. This is how it has evacuated from its disciplinary field the issue of the political origin of the crisis of measure, becoming *economics* after being born as *political economy*. The current crisis of economic indicators reveals how economic science is insufficient for analysing the transformations taking place today. This insufficiency derives from the very "mission" of economics—from its goal of eliminating the political analysis of power, and of power's effects on micro- and macroeconomic variables, from the field of inquiry.

But the "place for the socks" and the crisis of measure it reflects reveal two other things, equally crucial to the current paradigm of transformation.

In the sphere of domestic labor, we are dealing with a kind of labor that is becoming central to the post-Fordist regime. It is *live labor*, where "the product is inseparable from the producer." This labor, which achieves its own realization *within itself*, characterizes all forms of personal service. It continues to expand its reach in the directly productive sphere in the form of relational activities.

This labor is prevalently live labor because, as is evident in the domestic sphere, machinery (constant capital) is less important than personal work. While it's certainly true that the twentieth century has seen technology entering the household and rendering less cumbersome a whole series of domestic tasks (like laundry work), it is equally true that these technologies have not at all reduced the quantity of live labor performed by women. This paradoxical state of affairs has been demonstrated many times by research on technological innovation's effects on domestic work. The existence of household appliances such as washing machines has not reduced the quantity of live labor; in fact, there has been an increase. This is because the values and the aesthetic and cultural standards involved (the quest for ever more cleanliness, order, and so on) have led women to expand the forms of domestic labor in multiple ways. Instead of bathing the children once a week, we now do this every day. The husband changes his shirt every day. The effect is that of increasing the quantity of female labor.

Technology has simplified or eliminated a whole series of physically demanding activities, but the sociocultural context has caused an increase in the quantity and the quality of live domestic labor. Simply by virtue of being both an element and an effect of a certain sociocultural context, live labor has assumed a series of characteristics that are becoming increasingly typical of a communicational and relational kind of labor: by washing and ironing shirts once every two days instead of every ten days (as was done when the standards of cleanliness were less demanding), the wife or partner reinterprets, through her labor, the extra-familial *relational needs* of her husband and children. Her labor reproduces the very possibility of maintaining these external social *relations*. It is impossible to let the husband leave the house wearing the same shirt two days in a row, as this would mean jeopardizing his image and his class status.

Live domestic labor therefore reproduces in the private sphere a public relational context. This is precisely why it is an increasingly *communicative* and symbolic kind of labor, based on the signs, images, and representations of a specific sociocultural context. In order to be communicative, a woman's domestic activities require an increase in cognitive qualities; she needs to constantly interpret and *translate* into live labor the *signs* and the *information* coming from the context in which the family lives. She decides whom to invite for dinner and what meal to serve in order to "meet expectations," elaborates relational strategies geared towards the improvement of her husband's career prospects, invests in a network of sociocultural relations to guarantee an environment favorable to her children's education. In this way, live labor becomes less and less material in the mechanical-executive sense and more and more relational and communicative. This does not reduce the quantity of labor, but rather *modifies its very substance*.

The quantity of live labor does not diminish. It has actually increased, thereby contradicting all those theories of technological development that establish a relationship of linear causality between technological innovation and necessary labor. The incorporation of science into machinery or constant capital allows for the elimination of the *industrial* part of labor, the part that is material, operative and mechanical. Parallel to the reduction of industrial labor, there is an increase in the communicative and relational work that resorts to the cognitive and interpretative qualities of the people working in a certain context. The fatigue caused by communicative and relational labor is no longer purely physical, but involves the brain, as demonstrated by the proliferation of new pathologies associated with work-related *stress*.[10]

It is not surprising, then, that during the last few years the focus of women's struggle has "shifted" from mobilization for the right to equality to less visible but no less significant and effective forms of struggle. Relational dynamics, and hence language, are what is crucial in the new struggles. This shift only seems to mark a defeat with regard to male-female equality on the labor market. Of course, the inequality in compensation has not diminished; it has actually increased where other factors (conjunctural, ethnic, migratory) have intervened. Women were the first to be affected by the recession; they were pushed back behind what they had obtained during the phase of economic expansion.

Nevertheless, it needs to be pointed out that the "exodus" *from* wage labor—that is, from the very site of wage discrimination— often began *before* the recession, as has been demonstrated by research conducted in the United States during the 1980s. According to some researchers, the increase in the average number of children per woman can be *partially* explained in terms of the "retreat" into the private sphere that took place when the "long march" across the labor market didn't fulfill its promises.

It is certainly very difficult to establish causal relations in such a complex universe. Nonetheless, the hypothesis can be advanced that, faced with an aggravation of wage inequalities between men and women, or in any case with their persistence (constitutional rights notwithstanding), the shift to the relational and communicative terrain reveals not so much a defeat as a genuine innovation in the tools of feminist struggle. If domestic labor is indeed increasingly of a relational and communicative nature, then perhaps the choice of *language* as the place for defining female identity and difference originates in this mutation. In any case, the persistence of domestic labor explains why women preceded men in developing forms of antagonism proper to the field of linguistic and relational communication.

Language, the *ability* to communicate, is in fact far more universal than the rights inscribed in the constitution. The difference consists in the fact that the universality of rights such as the right to parity is purely formal. As such, it has to contend with the reality of power relations in everyday life, be it at work or in the home. Formal rights are quickly detached from people when we enter the universe of work and the immediate private relationships between men and women. Language, on the other hand, displays a peculiar feature that distinguishes it from formal rights: while it is also public and universal in nature (like constitutional rights), language is never detached from people. It always "transcends" the reality of personal power relations; it is an immanent resource that can be tapped into every time one needs to redefine one's identity and difference with respect to the other that gives orders. Language is the "place" where we can best conjugate the I and the We, the singular and the collective, the private and the public. In the case of feminine language and communication, what is genuinely new compared to more traditional forms of struggle is the fact that the public sphere *immediately constitutes* a political community.

As Ida Dominijanni points out, the far-reaching political innovation resides

[...] in the forms that we choose for our speech and for our silence, for changing reality or to interpret a changing reality: to intervene in politics or to build social ties. We have never adopted the same forms, the same gestures and the same words used in the politics of men. Often we have been told that we didn't speak or we didn't do enough: the truth is that we acted and we spoke in a different way. [...] The feminine revolution is like this, it doesn't follow either the parties or the classical modes of visibility and conflict. We haven't lost sight of the enemy: we often find him elsewhere than under his classical masks. We have not lost our speech according to a "prudent strategy of retreat": but we don't do politics with press-conferences, and for the most part not even with street demonstrations. The words of women are just at hand, for anyone wanting to listen: in the homes and in the factories, in parliaments, in the unions, in the parties, in the newspapers.

It hardly needs to be added that here

[...] the stakes are not limited to women, but involve the paradigms of transformation, the realism of utopia. Politics is not played on the table of governments, but in the field of interpretation.[11]

3. Value in the Information Economy

With the first signs of economic recovery—during 1991 in the United States and at the beginning of 1994 in Europe and Japan— it seemed clear that the end of the recession would modify certain fundamental economic relations. One in particular has been discussed practically everywhere: the relationship between investment and employment. The expression "growth without jobs"[12] has quickly become a slogan capable of inspiring both hope and fear: those who lost their job during the recession feared not finding a new one, and those who felt liberated from the obligation to work hoped to change their lives in a fundamental manner. The ambivalence of the expression "growth without jobs" needs to be questioned without resorting to simplifications and independently from enthusiasm and anxiety.

One thing is certain: the application of information technology changes the very nature of the *relationship* between investment and occupation, in the sense that the causal linearity that has always linked them is *rescinded*. This means that a certain volume of investment can lead *either* to a reduction *or* to an increase in the rate of employment. The *significance* of this relationship is not given *a priori*, but rather depends on the choice—made by entrepreneurs, the unions, or the state—of creating jobs that establish a proportion between the volume of wealth to be produced and the *kind* of occupation created.

Ever since the discovery of the "visible physical quantity" that a group of engineers working for the Bell corporation in 1942–43 called "information," we know we are facing a new dimension of matter.[13] Norbert Wiener, one of the fathers of cybernetics, defined information in negative terms: "Information is neither mass nor energy: information is information." Speaking before the American Academy of Science, Boulding said: "Here is the third fundamental dimension of matter." Shannon developed a theory of information as a visible physical quantity that can be used in order to ensure a superior transmission of signals (we are in midst of the Second World War, and the Americans need to protect their naval traffic to Europe with informational systems).

Defined in these terms, information is the essence of the new productive technologies. The definition of this third dimension of matter is completely tautological: "Information is information."[14] In any case, the tautology is productive by virtue of the rules, the syntax, and the specific *software* that ensure the functioning of this strange linguistic machine. The machine functions on the basis of an elementary unit of information, the "bit" (binary digit). The bit isn't in any way a unit of "meaning." It is a unit that can assume either of two distinct values, normally 0 and 1. The meaning of this information is not determined *a priori*, but depends on the organization of the program and on the way the program is put to use by its operator.

Once information technology is applied to productive and distributive processes, the fluctuation of employment rates follows a logic different from the one that has traditionally determined the relationship between investment in machines and the creation of jobs related to the use of these machines. The spread of information technology renders the creation of jobs problematic because, as we have seen, it determines a crisis of the indicators traditionally used in economic forecasting.

On the one hand, the accelerated development of information technology is rapidly undermining the importance of the software program's physical or material container. *Hardware* prices are falling at a constant rate even as new software programs vertiginously increase the potential of information technology. This is enough to explode statistical indicators based on the relationship between the costs of fixed capital (machinery) and the financial volume of investments.

On the other hand, the *use* of the new technologies is anything but predetermined. A new computer can simply be used as a superior writing machine, but it can also become the basis for multiple and extremely productive applications. Everything depends on the kind of organization that is developed "around" the new technologies; it depends on the training programs available in primary schools and schools of engineering, and on the political decision to reduce labor costs, maintain the same rate of employment, or both (by reducing the number of full-time employees and resorting to outside or part-time workers). For now, the logic of this decision is *opportunist*: in some cases, it is convenient to lay off workers; in others, image-related reasons make it preferable to wait (today, this is the case in banking and in the insurance business); in still other situations, it is convenient to invest in networks that connect productive units scattered across the world, thereby creating jobs abroad rather than in the country of origin.

One example of the resulting uncertainty over investment strategies and their effects on employment is so-called *reengineering*,[15] the latest "trend" in management science.[16] Reengineering, which could also be termed "reconfiguration," consists in a radicial modification of a company's mode of operation: a breaking down of vertical organizational structures ("deverticalizaton") and a consistent application of those new forms of information technology (expert systems, videodiscs, telecommunications, and so on) that were previously employed only in a mechanical way, without structural transformation. Reengineering allows company managers to take full advantage of computers by rethinking the very organization of management, rather than simply introducing computers into pre-existing bureaucratic-administrative procedures, as in the past.

The term "reengineering" derives directly from the field of information technology; it was invented by Michael Hammer, a professor of computer science at the Massachusetts Institute of

Technology. Hammer was inspired to coin the term while teaching his customers how to use computers in order to improve company efficiency. The old software programs utilized in company management needed to be dismantled and rebuilt in order to fit newer and more powerful computers. The task was all the more urgent as everyone had purchased a computer at some point after the 1970s, but without obtaining significant returns in terms of efficiency. In many cases, the opposite was true: additional workers (computer experts) had to be hired. A new cost had arisen—one sustainable in times of plenty, but not in times of scarcity.

People soon realized that the old software programs combined certain *procedures* with an entire organization of labor (characterized, for example, by an excessive segmentation of the work process) and that this was precisely the cause of the inefficiency. Hence the enthusiasm for organizational rethinking: in some cases, this meant a straightforward "restructuring" of the company, that is, layoffs; in others, there resulted original forms of experimentation and innovation that eliminated hazardous or mindless jobs and reintegrated previously distinct functions (abolishing, for instance, the frontier between engineers and *marketing* specialists).

"Reengineering Makes Companies Efficient and Shows Workers the Door," headlined *The Wall Street Journal*, adding that millions of jobs might be eliminated in coming years. According to John Skerrit of Anderson Consulting, this might be the social question of the near future. Paradoxically, computers, once synonymous with modernity and efficiency, have become inefficient due to their mechanical and unintelligent utilization, and this has had negative repercussions on people's quality of life. As soon as profits began to dwindle, people appealed to techniques such as reengineering in order to reduce personnel—a sign of the shortsightedness of companies, and often of unions as well. Companies investing in the new technologies blindly reproduced the procedural defects that had existed prior to the introduction of computers. Unions failed to demand different and more desirable forms of work when it was still possible, and are now being punished with a net loss of work.

In some cases, the fiscal incentives meant to promote innovative industries produce effects contrary to what was intended: when it becomes more convenient to put capital to work rather than people, a situation results in which workers are laid off both by the companies producing computers and by those using them. If low-wage labor can easily be recruited, as it can in border regions, mechanization gives way to the extensive use of a labor force whose costs are lower than those of machinery ("Mexicanization"). And if the technical competency of migrant labor increases, as it has in past years, then it may happen that part-time workers are enlisted to mount extremely complicated *chips* in garages or overcrowded apartments, as is now the case in Silicon Valley.

Reengineering is simply one management technique among others, and it far from being applied in a linear way. Even its promoters admit to a failure rate of between 60 and 80 percent, in a situation where 69 percent of American and 75 percent of European companies are already undergoing their "reconfiguration." Absent a strategy that takes into consideration the multiplicity of factors involved, even the most intelligent use of information technology risks being totally ineffective.

A fundamental characteristic of the new technologies, on the basis of which investment strategies and their effects on the rate of employment can be analyzed, is the progressive loss of importance of fixed capital, or machinery, in the determination of economic *value*.

Nowadays nobody purchases Apple or IBM stocks on the basis of considerations about the material assets owned by these corporations. What counts is not the real estate or the machinery owned by a company, but its contacts and the potential inherent in its marketing network, the strength of its sales, the organizational abilities of its managers and the inventive capacity of its personnel.

These are the so-called "intangible" assets or goods, true *symbols*, for which we still don't have a statistical or financial measuring device. Since stocks are a symbol of ownership (of a part of the company's profits), and since the capital represented by stocks is also a system of symbols for the "ability to produce" wealth, we are witnessing a proliferation of symbols that endlessly mirror one another. As Alvin Toffler says, capital is rapidly becoming "super-symbolic."

The measurement of the intellectual capital of a company is only in its early stages, but there is already a "movement" of scholars who, having understood the pivotal role of knowledge and of immaterial labor in the "New Economy," are conducting field research in this area. Banks, for instance, have a strong need to know "the value of intangibles" (soft assets) associated with the companies that ask them for credit; companies, in turn, have to be in a position to calculate the value of their intellectual capital in order to create development strategies on a highly competitive market.[17]

The loss of importance of fixed capital in the determination of capital value—to the point where there now exists an entire literature on the "virtual enterprises" of a not-so-distant future—dramatically modifies the categories on which the study of economic value used to be based. "The value of tangible goods can disappear overnight. But how can we evaluate the intangibles?" This is the question raised by Rob Petersen, vice president of the Canadian Imperial Bank of Commerce.

First of all, value is extracted during the entire production/delivery process of a commodity/service.[18] The post-Fordist economy is not characterized by the fact that people have suddenly decided to satisfy their needs with immaterial goods, but by the increasing integration of the activities pertaining to the economic sphere. The basic premises of the new production paradigm are connections rather than separations, forms of integration rather than of segmentation, real-time simultaneity rather than sequential phases. In other words, production neither starts nor ends in the factory. We can therefore affirm that productivity, as a measure of increases in economic value, begins even *before* the worker arrives in the office.

Indeed, in the evaluation/measurement of a company's intellectual capital, the central idea is that knowledge is both an intellectual and a relational material, both content and culture. It's not a matter of creating gigantic indicators, a sort of encyclopedia of knowledge similar to the one created by the philosophers of the Enlightenment, but rather of the elaboration of *maps* tracing a diffuse knowledge and allowing companies to find the "places" where knowledge is born, both inside and outside the factory. The objective is to keep a close eye on the people who remember the formulas, and then to develop the technologies that will "make them talk." According to Arian Ward, a theorist of business engineering, "people think in terms of stories, not of facts." This is why we need to draft maps capable of retracing the "song lines" described by Bruce Chatwin in his account of Australian aborigines: roads, trails, conduits of informal wisdom, "highways of knowledge," metaphors referring to other metaphors, the places where those original pieces of information needed in order to differentiate oneself on an increasingly homologizing market lie hidden.

According to the world's first "director of intellectual capital," Leif Edvinson of Scandinavian Assurance and Financial Services, "our financial assets stay here after 5 o'clock, but a good part of our intellectual capital goes back home."

The specific working activity occurring during the productive process is therefore impossible to measure by traditional criteria. The classic definition of productivity, which relates the value of the finished product to the cost of the factors of production (labor and/or invested capital), no longer has any operational meaning. This criterion of measure was effective in a time when telecommunications, services, and immaterial technologies were neither as diffuse nor as decisive as they are today. Now we are witnessing the birth of "cognitive laborers," a class of producers no longer "commanded," to use Adam Smith's terminology, by machines external to live labor, but rather by technologies that are increasingly mental, symbolic, and communicative. The new fixed capital, the new machine that commands live labor and makes the worker produce, is no longer a physically identifiable and specifically situated tool, but tends rather to be located within the worker herself, in her brain and in her soul.

This means that the new form of fixed capital is constituted by a network of social and vital relations, by the ways in which production and information are first acquired and later, after coalescing in labor force, activated in the production process. The progressive dematerialization of the modes of production is accompanied by a sort of *spatialization* of the sociocultural resources that combine in the composition of "cognitive laborers," the class constituted by post-Fordist immaterial producers. Any social context can become the fixed capital whose combination with live labor makes that live labor productive, and therefore competitive at the international level.

In fact, the human resource of intellectuality is the true origin of value, but this origin amounts to nothing if it isn't captured and transformed into a company asset. This calls for the elaboration of intellectual *structures*, such as information systems, which provide channels of knowledge and constitute the medium for consumer relations. These systems are the basis for the reproduction of the "cartography," for the interaction among different kinds of information. According to the formula developed by Dave Ulrich, a professor at the University of Michigan, "learning capacity equals g times g," that is, it is equal to a company's ability to generate new ideas, multiplied by the company's ability to generalize those ideas.

Productivity cannot be measured on the basis of the quantity of goods produced per hour, nor can it be determined by reference to a specific company or economic sector. What is measured, instead, is a multiplicity of factors characterizing a social and regional space that transcends the single worker and allows her to create wealth by being *a member of a community*. It is therefore no paradox that the same companies where people are studying how to better measure the value of intangibles have suppressed their internal adjournment workshops. It isn't only a matter of (enormous) costs whose benefits are difficult to quantify, but of a new strategy of diffusion/accumulation, which plays out in increasingly *informal* ways. The employees can study written materials, consult their colleagues, or take classes, if they want; what really counts for the company is evaluating the *development* of its human capital, not the amount of money spent on *training* classes. The real evaluation consists in the "social validation" of the intellectual capital developed, that is, in the degree of customer *satisfaction* that can be translated into sales volume. As is only normal, it is at the moment of *sale* that the human resources activated in the production process are monetized and therefore measured. As abstract value *par excellence*, money sanctions the value of human capital, "reducing it to a commodity," revealing its market inadequacies, and providing information—comparable to inventory data—on where and how to intervene in order to better adapt production to market demand.

One consequence is that investment decisions made on a purely company-based calculation, such as decisions intended to reduce direct compensation or social benefits (indirect compensation) in order to respond to ferocious international competition, risk exposing the company to a "boomerang effect." The company may benefit in the short term, but in the medium and long term such decisions contribute to the destruction of the sociocultural context in which the company is inscribed, and which is at the very basis of its productive capacity. The accounting methods still common today treat the "brick and mortar" owned by the company as a capital asset, but refuse to consider intellectual capital as an expense![19]

The investment strategies and incentives elaborated by communities in order to promote investment are increasingly based on the growth of the "sociocultural machinery," of the identity-building "cognitive capital" capable of producing wealth when it comes into contact with live labor. It is also clear that a company is not innovative simply because it invests in advanced technologies: neither technology as such, nor even the "trendiest" management models are capable of ensuring local or regional development. The only innovations truly deserving of social incentives are those promoting the development of the social cognitive capital that is tapped into by each particular company according to its own preferred modalities of development.

4. Spaces of Interpretation

The crisis in the measure of value was obviously bound to reverberate within the different theories of compensation which, from the end of the 1970s onward, have been proposed in order to explain or legitimate certain choices in the compensation policies adopted at the company level. The gradual spread of post-Fordism has caused a complete reversal in the understanding of compensation: compensation is no longer understood as the price of labor power determined by the application of a specific rule (that of supply and demand), but rather as the result of an *interpretive act* that concerns a set of *rules*. This radical change of perspective is inscribed in the new way in which most economic problems are now treated: economic theory's center of gravity has shifted from the market to the company. The impossibility of foreseeing everything, the volatility typical of post-Fordism, has put into question traditional models of unlimited rationality, forcing us to define *restricted* fields of rational calculation (limited rationality).

The collective research project "Working Under Different Rules," conducted by the National Bureau of Economic Research under the direction of American economist and Harvard professor Richard B. Freeman, has underscored the decisive role of rules and institutions in labor market dynamics by means of a comparative study of North America (United States and Canada), Europe, and Japan. The results of the study can be summarized as follows:

> 1. During the 1980s, the discrepancy in compensation increased everywhere, but only in the United States did we witness a consistent decline in "real" wages, particularly in the area of unskilled labor. In the United States, job creation has

been made possible by poverty rates that are significantly higher than those of Europe and Japan.

2. Worker representation at the company level (worker commissions) or in specific economic sectors has seriously declined in the United States. In countries like Germany and Canada, worker commissions have proved to be "resilient" institutions, capable of resisting even in periods characterized by a crisis of collective bargaining and a marked loss of trade union power (although in Canada these commissions are concerned only with issues such as health insurance and work safety).

3. In the United States, employees have less access to in-company professional training than in Europe and Japan. In the United States, there is a preference for *learning by doing*.[20] While it increases short-term productivity, this strategy is inadequate in the long term.

4. In the compensation pyramid, the lower class of American workers has a standard of living far below that of the corresponding European and Japanese workers. The social security network does not provide a sufficient income for the lower strata of the American population. The increase of American poverty rates with respect to those of other economically advanced countries occurred between the end of the 1970s and the beginning of the 1980s.

5. The different dynamics typical of the United States and of other advanced nations can be traced to variations in the capacity of labor institutions to intervene in the determination of wages and influence the quality of training. The role of the state in guaranteeing an adequate level of training has proven to be essential in every country with the exception of the United States.

6. The comparison of the various countries examined shows that effective labor representation at the company level is possible only when it is adequately supported by labor *legislation*.

7. The preservation of the welfare state is essential for reducing the inequalities in gross compensation created by the market economy, that is, for improving the distribution of available profits. This improvement always implies a cost to the community, either in fiscal or in deficit terms.

8. Social intervention has modest effects on the functioning of the job market, especially when redistribution measures are directly or indirectly related to policies designed to reintegrate workers into the world of labor.

9. The inequalities in the different levels of education and training strongly contribute to the aggravation of inequalities in the distribution of income. Policies aimed at increasing the supply of qualified labor force start positive processes in the quest for increasing income through retraining.

10. Guaranteeing an adequate income to the less qualified sectors of labor helps preserve occupational opportunities for the long-term unemployed. While this income is lowest in the United States, that country also has a lower rate of unemployment.

11. Those European countries (mainly Great Britain) that tried to make their job market more flexible by following the example of the American "model" during the 1980s have not been able to vanquish unemployment in any significant way.

At this point, the question needs to be raised whether the "virtues" of the European and Japanese social systems—which, the researchers conclude, the United States should adopt in order to break out of the spiral "job-creation/pauperization"—can actually survive under a post-Fordist and strongly globalised economic regime.

In all European countries, the recession of the early 1990s has been used to impose *American-style*[21] deregulation. The strategy of making employment more flexible in order to respond to market fluctuations in real time is adopted in order to reduce wages and increase the specific productivity of labor. Harassed by an entrepreneurial class that wants them to contain the cost of income replacement (and in particular that of unemployment compensation), the European welfare states can only redirect social intervention towards the goal of guaranteeing a survival income, even if this is only possible by the kind of social mobilization that has occurred in France. What is more, the struggle against structural unemployment is only possible if the communicative and relational activities associated with personal services are legitimated in socioeconomic terms.

From the point of view of the relation between direct and indirect compensation, the deregulation of the job market brings to the fore the issue of recuperating productivity gains for pensions, disability insurance, and unemployment benefits. According to a study conducted in Germany by McKinsey Consultants, reducing both labor costs and the financial pressure of social programs without increasing long-term unemployment requires a significant expansion of part-time work.[22]

McKinsey's analysts write that achieving both more flexible forms of production and productivity gains requires reducing labor time for an increasing number of active workers (around 60 percent of the total work force). The study shows that work productivity can increase between 3 and 20 percentage points when labor time is reduced thanks to an increase in personal *output*,[23] a more elastic management of demand fluctuations, and an extension of the life span of companies. Work productivity can also expand as a result of a higher motivation to work and a reduction of *stress* and absenteeism.

In the strategy of generalizing part-time work, the transfer of productivity gains is crucial. McKinsey estimates that a 25 percent reduction in labor time should not imply a salary reduction greater than 15 percent, especially in the case of low-wage workers, for whom it is essential that the state guarantees the minimum for survival. What is more, in order to be effective, this model must guarantee the possibility of returning to full-time employment, and the choice to reduce one's working hours must not increase the risk of being laid off when the company wants to reduce its workforce.

Whatever one thinks of the model presented by McKinsey, it is important to underscore that combining flexibility, productivity, and labor cost reduction requires a reduction in working hours. Furthermore, the guarantee of a wage reduction less than proportional to the reduction in hours worked introduces the notion of rules established by the company, the employees, and the welfare state. These are rules which need to include the subjects populating the universe of subcontracting, if one wants to avoid a situation in which resistance to lower wages is responded to by *outsourcing*.[24] Absent these subjects, *the interpretation* of the rules would be incomplete from the very beginning.

Rules and their interpretation are, indeed, the two terms which characterize the most recent income theories.[25] In describing the interpretation of the local and general rules guiding the determination of parameters utilized to calculate total income, productivity rates, and job security, these theories affirm the centrality of the notion of "cognitive dissonance." For the rules to be interpreted correctly, it is necessary to define the *spaces* where these rules can be interpreted by all parties concerned. While it is true that a rule only exists to the extent to which it is applied, it is also true that the application of a rule requires interpretation, and therefore the possibility for the multiple subjects participating in the definition of the rule to express the knowledge that defines their specific identity.

In other words, the deregulation of the job market calls forth the notion of a space of interpretation, understood as a place for negotiation that is absolutely essential if we want to avoid negative, *American-style* consequences for the labor force. Thus defined, compensation becomes a mechanism for the distribution of collective knowledge, a knowledge that needs to be made explicit by the negotiating subjects in order for them to be able to interpret the proposed rules.

In this movement towards the opening of spaces for interpretation, we can retrace the effort to avoid a development in which the linguistic turn of the economy is not accompanied by a no less crucial redefinition of the spaces and the modalities of wage negotiation. Instrumental and communicative action should coincide not just in the field of commodity and service production, but also in the space where social relations are reproduced, the space where knowledge and income are distributed.

3

State and Market

1. The Limits of Clintonism

In 1991, less than one year before Bill Clinton's election to the United States presidency, the economist Robert Reich published *The Work of Nations*. This book was to be a decisive politico-economical contribution to what would later be defined as *Clintonomics*, a transition program from Fordism to post-Fordism after twelve years of neoliberal policies. Reich's nomination as Secretary of Labor in the new administration further confirms the weight carried by his theses in the elaboration of Clinton's strategies.

Crucial to the entirety of Reich's analysis is the role of immaterial labor in the post-Fordist era, both as the basis of a renewed American power on the global scene, and for the reconstruction of a political and social caste able to replace the middle class that had disintegrated during the 1980s. This was the same resentful and fearful class that had allowed Ross Perot to gain almost 20 percent of the votes in 1992.

Immaterial work, the activity consisting in the "manipulation of symbols"—to use Reich's expression—only represents one side of Clintonism. The other side, which is of equal importance, is the redefinition of the Welfare State, the social State that needs to know how to manage post-Fordist growth while keeping an eye on the cost of healthcare and social programs. The United States, whose health system is 60 percent private, spends twice as much as countries whose system is 70 to 80 percent public. In fact, Americans spend three times more, *pro capita*, than what people pay in France, and all they have to show for it is an inefficient and unjust system that excludes 35 million people. The transformation of the American health system toward a public model would imply an immediate reduction in the price of medicines, doctors' compensations and hospital costs—three sectors whose prices in the United States reach record levels. This will make the acceptance of the reform plan directed by Hillary Clinton extremely problematic, curtailing its reach and diluting it over time.[1]

Clintonism also defined itself against the wave of Perot's supporters, much more so than against the Republicans. According to Ross Perot, the crucial issue for the United States is the federal budget, and not the decline of American cities or the poverty of millions of Americans. In fact, Clinton won the elections because Perot stole from Bush the votes coming from the suburbs inhabited by retirees and the employees of the high-tech corporations that are also housed there. On his own, Clinton obtained a consensus 3 percent lower than the one enjoyed by Dukakis in 1988. Perot's supporters favor tax reductions and cuts in public spending, especially for urban areas. The depressed inner cities, which during the Los Angeles riots had revealed to the entire world the real consequences of Reaganism, were not a concern for a Democratic party that was placing its bets on the white population employed in the service sector, also housed in the suburbs (the *suburban majority*) and already worried by the employment crisis.

The politico-institutional geometry emerging from this entanglement of diverging perspectives risks exasperating the *spatial apartheid* caused by the move towards the suburbs on the part of businesses and corporations. In the last ten years, the American urban centers lost 30 percent of their jobs, while the suburbs have seen a 25 percent increase. The ethnic separations of urban spaces has dramatically polarized income levels: while in 1980, the individual income in urban areas was 90 percent of the one in the suburbs, in 1990 it only reached 59 percent. In order to resist the "Perotist" front, the democratic administration is forced to destine public investments to the construction of extremely expensive railway systems, fiber-optic networks and interstate highways that will essentially benefit the suburb-based Perot's electorate, as are the white-owned construction firms.

Clinton's programs have generally been interpreted from an economic point of view as if we were dealing with "the return of Keynes" (and of Kennedy), without taking into consideration the social, ethnic and territorial decomposition of the last two decades. But we cannot ignore the sociopolitical reshuffling of the American society generated by Reagan's policies, and that Ross Perot has somehow revealed in his populist crusade. The spatial distribution of votes, with the minorities dominating the inner cities and the mostly white middle class in the suburbs, forces the public administration to selectively assign the distribution of public funds. The "Perot effect," with its emphasis on deficit reduction, in fact makes an economic analysis of Clintonism quite unnecessary. More than a Keynesian State intervention, we are witnessing a form of economic and political engineering, a not necessarily coherent array of measures aimed at circumscribing the different conflicts traversing the United States.

It is certain, though, that with Bill Clinton and his team, industrial policies reclaim their centrality after a decade dominated by finance and debt-fueled consumption. The crucial role of the enterprise is founded on the theory of *endogenous development* proposed mainly by the Nobel-prize winning economist Ronald Coase and later by Paul Romer and Robert Reich. According to this theory, the interactions between economic actors don't necessarily occur through the markets. There are *externalities*—positive (such as education) or negative (environmental degradation)—that constitute *additional* costs and benefits not included in market transactions. The collectivity is ultimately responsible for regulating these externalities, thereby legitimizing State intervention, because only the State is able to take into consideration collective priorities. In other words, public intervention is justified because the spontaneous balance constituted by the sum of private initiatives does not create an optimal collective equilibrium.

There is no doubt that the environmental disasters caused by the wild deregulation policies of the 1980s are the historical context for this economic theory. The market's "invisible hand" is in fact perfectly recognizable in naval and aviation tragedies, as well as in deforestation and water pollution problems. These are concrete signs of the market's failure, but paradoxically they have been addressed by trying to "marketize" what the market alone can't control. We are putting a price tag (as "property rights") on the use of environmental resources in order to discourage excessive use or, symmetrically, to encourage their responsible utilization.

Beyond the environmental question, the theses of these American economists have been reinforced by the analysis of the inequalities in income distribution and education. According to the research of "urban economists" such as Paul Romer, the polarization between rich and poor inherited from the Reagan years is actually working *against* economic growth. This is an important reversal of the conventional wisdom, according to which only a rapid and unimpeded economic growth can create the conditions for a better income distribution and thence a decrease in inequality. Until recently, we seemed to think that inequality is the *result*, and not the *cause*, of slow growth.

In fact, everything seems to tell us that the origin of the slow growth characteristic of the beginning of the 1990s is to be found in the extreme disparity between rich and poor. In a "domino effect," this disparity has encouraged behaviors that run contrary to what would be desirable for the functioning of the market economy (demotivation among the unemployed and in the school population, dealing drugs as a way of countering the lack of income sources in the urban centers).

For the Clinton administration, the inefficacy of deregulation from the point of view of economic growth is all the more alarming given that it had strategically invested its resources in the development of infrastructures supporting the development of new technologies. The deterioration of professional education caused by social inequalities and the absence of rules aimed at protecting the sociocultural environment threatens any program aimed at relaunching the United States in the global arena. In fact, one can invest any amount of money in education without obtaining any significant results if the disparity in income and opportunities persists or worsens.

The American economist James O'Connor said that at the origin of Reaganism's triumphs and failures was the land itself.[2] The land and the work force are goods that, in an increasingly globalized economy characterized by industry's migration towards countries with low wage costs, *stay at home*. In the Reagan years, the land has been the object of very significant real estate and financial speculations, as well as fiscal deals. Most of all, the land has been the "place" of growth for services of every kind, creating poorly paid and nonunionized jobs (76 percent of jobs are service related, and 42 percent of them are low-wage). According to O'Connor, with Reagan and the President George H. W. Bush, the rent derived from real estate deals has become even more important than salaries and profits.

In this context, we are no longer talking about industrial policies, but of *a political economy of the land.* These are policies valorizing the interdependence between industry and land. In the "industrial Keynesianism" serving as backdrop for the Clinton administration, the service sector is deemphasized to the advantage of the most advanced industries. This makes it impossible to structurally intervene on the social, ethnic and racial imbalances caused by the economic exploitation typical of the service sector. In other words, if it is true that behind the centrality of the corporation lies the "immaterial labor" analyzed by Robert Reich, it is also true that there is no clear vision on how to territorialize or spatially organize this kind of labor. The State is given the task of managing the endogenous development and the synergies existing between individual investment and collective productivity, but this can only be done by territorializing immaterial labor. This passage is made inescapable by the fusion between industry and service sector in an economy where industry functions more and more as a service provider and vice versa. It is impossible to support only one of these poles without endangering the other. The technology industries and the social and cultural resources that surround them feed on each other. This is the main aporia of Clintonism.

Already in Reich's study it was clear how the post-Fordist economic paradigm was the victim of a certain "sociological reductionism" insofar as a perfectly reasonable critique of the classical economical categories of primary, secondary and tertiary production ended up producing a new tripartite fallacy: repetitive (taylorized) work, service work, and immaterial work (for the producers of symbols). According to Reich, it is the fruits of intellectual labor that are truly important for a nation: scientific and technological research, education of the work force, improvement in management techniques, new communication technologies and digitalized financial networks. In the universe of intellectual labors we find: researchers, engineers, programmers, lawyers, creative accountants, management consultants, financial advisors, advertisers, publishers, journalists and university professors. This "caste" is destined to accelerate the loss of prestige suffered by all taylorist (repetitive and applied) activities, that can be performed in countries where the work force is less expensive. On the other hand, services to the people, while important in an aging society increasingly dependent on tertiary assistance, will not be rewarded financially because in Reich's vision they are not creative activities.

The gist of Reich's theories is the following: economic globalization makes it impossible to speak of capital ownership in terms of the national composition of the means of production. A Ford car, for instance, is the result of partial and combined activities dispersed on the entire planet and devised within global webs where efficiency and productive communication are all that matters. The automobile resulting from this process is a composite of parts produced in different countries on the basis of multinational capital.

On the other hand, what is lost as a consequence of capital denationalization (that is, as a consequence of the means of production and of constant capital), is regained by the property of immaterial labor as a control over the production of knowledge. The denationalization of physical-material capital is contrasted with

the nationalization of knowledge and the command on its organization. From now on, "buying American" will mean "valorizing
American knowledge." Nationality, still according to Reich, is recu-
perated when we strategically invest in the most valued
activities—that is, the immaterial activities that irradiate the post-
Fordist mode of production. Therefore, we need to nationalize the
income generated through immaterial activities as a way to com-
pensate for the unemployment of the nonspecialized American
work force (which is now competing with emerging countries) and
to reduce the income gap between professionals and the working
poor without diminishing the position of the United States in the
global economy. American pride should function as cohesive agent:
the increased wealth produced by the productivity and the higher
qualifications of immaterial labor with respect to other countries
will give us the fiscal resources to alleviate the deterioration in the
living conditions of the non-qualified American population.

The fault in this kind of reasoning consists in the individuation
of a particular *caste* as an economic and political *leader* on the basis
of its added value, thereby preserving the same connotations of the
Fordist era, and notably the tripartite structure of the Statist
structuring of the job market. This is why Reich assigns immaterial
labor to the spaces of residential suburbs and academic campuses,
which are precisely the spaces of the classist *apartheid* that in the last
two decades has exasperated the disaggregation of American society.
Why should the caste of immaterial workers agree to renounce its
wealth in order to ameliorate the lot of those Americans that have
been reduced to living in Third World conditions? What would be
the source of solidarity, given that the very definition of this caste is
founded on spatial, cultural and even racial exclusion? Nationalism?
But why should a broker, or a professional researcher, living in a Los

Angeles or New York residential neighborhood feel more American than his Swiss colleagues living in Zurich's gated communities? The denationalization of capital can't logically lead to the nationalization of immaterial labor. It is hard, then, to see how the American people could actually enjoy the advantages that advanced countries detain with respect to the emerging economies, which possess cheap raw materials but not a professionally qualified workforce. Everything seems to run against a renewed role of the Nation-State: nationalism certainly does not go in the direction of the protection of the weak, the unemployed, the non-qualified American workers, young people lost in the job market and drug trafficking, or the multiethnic immigrants.

We have to be clear about the fact that the definition of work within the post-Fordist regime is not an academic question, and that it can't be reduced to a *querelle* between sociologists. It is a fundamental issue that is at the very basis of the political strategies and international conflicts of the next few years.

It is true that economic globalization forces developed countries to focus their attention on comparative advantages, that is, on opposing the higher qualifications and productivity of immaterial workers to the material growth of emerging economies.[3] It is also true that the combination of technological innovation and the increase in imported goods from emerging countries is at the origin of the destruction of non-qualified jobs and the widening of income disparities in rich countries. What we don't know is whether, "in the long run," this transition will allow rich countries to regain high growth rates on the basis of their comparative advantages (the productivity of immaterial labor) and emerging countries to consolidate their economic strength on the basis of their current comparative advantages (non-qualified workforce, or qualified but low cost).

In this context, the weak link is represented by international debt. On the international scene, this is, more or less, the way immaterial labor functions: in Vietnam or Thailand a famous designer buys for three dollars a shirt conceived in Paris or Zurich. The shirt will be sold in the West for forty-five dollars in the name of the "immaterial" designer. Thanks to patents, trademarks and intellectual property—that is, to the much higher remuneration commanded by knowledge with respect to material-applied labor—wealth is in fact redistributed to the North. But the South, while benefiting from exporting the goods it agrees to produce to the North, also has to rely on the credit of the richer countries, not so much to finance the acquisition of the means of production (this is the job of the liberalized capital markets, which are now increasingly focused on emerging countries), but to acquire the *know-how*, the knowledge encapsulated in the goods and services coming from the North. As a consequence, with the exacerbation of international debt caused by the centrality of immaterial labor, the countries of the South will continue to function as immigration sources for the North. The improvement in the education level of the new immigrants, achieved through the higher rates of development in the South, will allow corporations of the North to also exploit the South *within* the class of immaterial workers, taking advantage of highly qualified clandestine labor and using racism as a way of favoring the citizens of the Northern nations.

The class definition of immaterial labor is doubly wrong: it does not take into consideration real global dynamics and it is politically weak. This is all the more true considering the obstacles encountered by the Clinton administration in its projects for reforming the welfare state (the example of health reform will suffice). These obstacles are raised precisely by the social class strategically courted by Clinton during the elections, when he tried to forge a new center in order not to lose too many voters to Ross Perot. This social class is politically opposed to any attempt to redistribute equally the profits of the American economic growth because its livelihood depends on it and also because it feels productive *as a consequence* of the segmentation and exclusivity of immaterial labor. The result of this dynamic is that the redefinition of the United States' hegemonic role in terms of immaterial labor ends up *reproducing at home* the North/South polarization.

The transition to post-Fordism needs a social State that is able to manage the decomposition of the old Fordist regime with its effects on non-qualified labor and the precarization of labor that accompanies it. Clinton understood this new role, and this gave him the support of more advanced American capital, notwithstanding the scandals that, just a few years earlier, would have caused the withdrawal of equally qualified candidates. But the construction of a social state adequate to this transition needs strong political alliances, able to resist the attacks of the most privileged sectors of society which oppose any form of fiscal redistribution of wealth and any investment in inner cities infrastructures that would improve the life conditions of ethnic minorities and the unemployed of any color.

The Clinton administration has implemented a weak strategy because its theoretical-political premises were weak, particularly its definition of immaterial workers as a social class, when in fact immaterial labor is founded on a spatial-territorial dimension that originates in the post-Fordist paradigm. Immaterial labor, based on the "manipulation of symbols, data and discourses," is only a part (a sector) of the much more diverse field of communicative-relational labor at the center of post-Fordist economies. Communicational-relational work happens throughout the whole circuit of production, distribution and reproduction, and it consists in multiple activities. Some are new, some are old; some are immaterial whereas others are artisanal, some are technologically advanced whereas others are traditional, some are language-based whereas others are purely operational and silent. Placing all political bets on a single sector within this field of activities means gravely endangering the success of any reformist platform.

In fact, the Clinton administration has found itself, two years after the elections, "improving security in every American neighborhood" with laws against criminality that are just an aggravation of the repressive measures enacted against the poor populations of the urban ghettos, while the budget for crime prevention has been significantly cut. Through the facade of a "reform of public assistance," Clinton only succeeded in reducing the duration for receiving aid from the government to two years and cutting its amount, in order to encourage the poor to go back to an unstable and underpaid job market.[4] Clinton's reformism appears as a new version of the Republican welfare policies, with all the political and social risks that will inevitably accompany them. And as it always happens in American history, the limits of internal reforms are somehow "sublimated" in the characteristic interventionist zeal on the international arena.

2. The Idea of the Middle Class

Expressions such as "assault on the center," "center extremism" and "centrist alliances" when referring to governing strategies are the clearest demonstration that the post-Fordist transition has not only fractured the political and institutional balance of the years roughly from 1945 to 1975, but has also left a gap in our political categories. We are left without the analytical instruments that would allow us to dispel the feeling of confusion when we try to interpret our present.

Traditional parties, new social movements, and new political coalitions all meet grave difficulties in the definition of their programmatic strategies and institutional alliances, mainly because of the upheaval undergone by their electoral bases as a consequence of the transformation in the mode of production and in the mechanisms of wealth distribution. If the fall of the Berlin wall appeared to have dealt a decisive blow to "class society," what in fact emerged in the last few years is the quest for a political definition of the "third estate," of that ensemble of productive subjects who, although they "do everything," "have nothing." They have no power, and power does not represent them. As John Betjeman said: "This omnivorous element is now and will always be for us, as it has always been—*class*."

The class whose "substance" and "internal composition" we are looking for (in terms of employment, income, birth, spousal choices, education, "forms of expression," etc.) is of course, the *middle* class, and it could not have been otherwise. Indeed, it is on this class that rests the very possibility of *governing* a society. It is obvious that the "general interest" refers to the average of the particular interests crisscrossing a society, but representing such a middle class today is much less obvious. To represent means *to forcefully present*, to choose not only a lens, but an image: this, of course, implies that the middle class is socially *visible*.[5]

But today more than ever, the middle class whose electoral support is so desperately wanted cannot easily be defined by traditional criteria and sociopolitical indicators; quite the contrary: the instruments normally used in the various social sciences all point to the crisis, if not the disappearance, of this very class. Statistically, it is crystal clear that during the transition from Fordism to post-Fordism the class that suffered the most from the restructuration of production and income polarization has been the "class in between," the class that, throughout Fordism, had found an occupational and social stability that made its behavior and political allegiances largely predictable.

In this respect, too, the instruments that we have today for economic indicators don't tell us anything but simply mirror their own inadequacy. However, this does not prevent the current transformation to exploit *the concept, the image,* of a "middle class." We could in fact say that the more a middle class is socially and economically *impossible to synthesize,* the more it is politically demanding and active in the creation of its own "agitators" and "leagues." Today the middle class is an "impossible class," but it is intractable all the same. This might be why everyone wants to represent it.

In any case, there is a debate on the concept of the middle class whose origins are very remote and whose terms remind us of the old "controversy" between Marx and the social utopists, particularly with respect to the distinction between *technical and political class composition.* Then as now, the technological processes of restructuration had created new professions, eliminating many traditional occupations. The essential political problem was the analysis of the kind of relation between capital and labor that resulted from these processes, of the command by capital of an increasingly socialized and integrated labor, and of the form of the political-institutional representation of this class re-articulation.

We all remember that the workers in the English cotton mills, led by their "aristocracies" and "little masters," were the ones who demanded universal suffrage. The *Reform Act* of 1832 was a victory of the industrial class and mid-level artisans and workers over the *Tory* government, which represented a British elite that since 1680 had frozen its own political institutions, rendering them impenetrable to any reformist idea and practice. The *Reform Act* was a masterpiece of strategic alliances between the party of the industry magnates (the Whigs) and industrial and agricultural workers: the workers wanted the right to vote, while the Whigs asked for a more equitable distribution of the electoral colleges in order to insure a fair representation in the greater industrial and commercial centers.

The electoral reform of 1832 was achieved thanks to the antigovernment mobilization of the social classes most directly threatened by the unstoppable diffusion of the factory system: the artisans, apprentices and small entrepreneurs who saw in the new systems of production the end of their autonomy. These were the subjects who, since the beginning of the century, had shown the strongest repulsion toward the degrading rules of the factory system and had resisted the loss of meaning of their work. Their activities were now becoming hetero-directed. The rhetoric of compensation and restoration, the defense of old rights and old forms of justice, generated new forms of militant struggles on the basis of the memory of an autonomy experienced before the advent of industrialization. These struggles helped the formation of a middle class composed of the "common people" described by John Stuart Mill as the "most cordial and virtuous in the community" and which he always claimed as his own. Lord Brougham, during the upheavals tied to the Reform Act, was inspired by the theory of the eminent virtues of the middle class, and Richard Codben used the expression "middle-class agitators" to describe a group of his allies in the Anti-Corn League.

In fact, the 1832 electoral reform insured an increase in the political power of the industrialists by granting more political weight to the populations of the industrial centers, but this was achieved at the expense of the so-called *rotten boroughs*, the underdeveloped areas that until then had been the electoral bases of the big land owners. The nature of the parties themselves was transformed, and they took new names, "conservative" and "liberal." The two-party system became the form of government of an industrialization based on new communication technologies (railways and steamboats), which allowed the steel and the heavy equipment industries to dominate the entire industrial structure, becoming the paradigm of the new model of production and distribution.

It is hard not to recognize in this politico-institutional juncture a strong resemblance to what is happening today in our post-Fordist societies. Zygmunt Bauman affirms in his *Memories of Class*:

> What made of the period in question an era of sharp conflicts, shifting alliances, consolidation of new divisions and, on the whole, an accelerating social change, was ultimately (to borrow Barrington Moore's cogent term) the sense of outraged justice on the part of those who justly felt their status withdrawn and the grounds of their security undermined. Paradoxically, the most profound re-articulation of society in human history derived its momentum from the hostility to change which spurred the impaired and the threatened into defensive (to wit, subjectively conservative) action. The intensity of militancy did not reflect the absolute level of destitution, but the distance between expectations and reality. Penury correlated but feebly with social protest. The rebels were sometime paupers— but more often than not they acted to stave off the spectre of indigence.[6]

The year after the electoral reform started the era of "factory inspections": the masses of the working class, composed of uprooted peasants and artisans forced to abandon their shops by capitalist competition, came to the forefront of history—they become the problem of the political relation between capital and labor, of the control, on a massive scale, on the struggle concerning compensation and working hours that gave birth to the first examples of social legislation. During this historic passage, we witness the end of the productive autonomy of the small entrepreneur, of the owner-director, of the capitalist-overseer, the socialist crisis (for the *utopian* socialists) of autonomous labor.

During this crisis, the historical memory of the autonomy of body and soul experienced in one's profession had become the glue holding together the resistance against the diffusion of the factory system. The crisis also allowed the rational utilization of work ethics in building systems of control over non-qualified workers and establishing an ethic of discipline. The factory system, which started with the women and children in the work houses and the poor in the hospices, soon extended well beyond the factory, modeling a system of disciplinary control that extended to the whole life of the working class (church, school, family). In its basic principles, this model perfectly corresponded to the Panopticon, the circular prison devised by Jeremy Bentham, the ideologue of utilitarianism and of the bourgeois Constitution, in order to insure a maximum of visibility.

The middle class was born in the transition from economic-productive autonomy to *capital's autonomy*, with its command of the processes of valorization and the production of wealth. It was born as a complex social category, full of resentment and traditionalist nostalgia, constantly asking to be compensated for the loss of the rights that it had acquired before the economic-institutional revolution. It is precisely the complexity inherent to the middle class that makes its unilateral definition impossible. As Philip N. Furbank has noted, the result is that "the idea that 'classes' can be defined by economic or material criteria, or in fact defined by any criteria at all, is a mistake."[7]

Marx himself speaks of classes not to identify them, but to *create them*. Marx's problem is to insure that the underprivileged think of themselves as a class: in order to do so, it's necessary to invent a *class enemy*, that is, another class—the bourgeoisie. These are "necessary fictions" that we need to make real and they are real only when they *act politically*. In this "language game," in this rhetorical definition of class (where "rhetorical" does not mean "unfounded," but rather, *politically founded*) we can in fact find the origin of the middle class, that *thinks itself as such in the reflection of its own self-given image*. Paraphrasing Proust in his considerations on the work of the writer, we can in fact say that the task of the politician is only a sort of optical instrument offered to the electorate so that it may see what, without a program, it would not have recognized in itself. And that politics is an art form is amply demonstrated by the example of those who built their power precisely on the rhetoric of the middle class.

The 1980s have shown how the middle class defined as an income bracket has gradually declined, as a consequence of the downward mobility experienced by white-collar workers, and that the crisis of this middle class is also the symptom of its qualitative mutation. The *dumpies* (downwardly mobile professionals according to the *Business Week* definition) have replaced the more widely known *yuppies*. In the United States, while at the beginning of the 1980s 90 percent of laid-off white-collar workers found a new position, by the end of the same decade that percentage decreased to 50 percent. At the beginning of the 1990s it has declined further to only 25 percent. The recession that started in 1989 has in fact been a white-collar recession, as it is clear in the 1993 Economic Report of the President elaborated by the Council of Economic Advisers for the Clinton administration. The relative proportion of white- and blue-collar unemployment has consistently increased since the beginning of the 1980s, to such an extent that already in 1992 80 percent of layoffs targeted white-collar workers.[8]

These trends, which are similar in all countries involved in the post-Fordist restructuration, can be explained on the one hand by the loss of importance of middle management in corporate structures (which is the result of the loss of verticality in corporate organization and the reaggregation of functions on the horizontal level), and on the other by the outsourcing of entire productive sectors, which lead not only to the layoff of many qualified professionals but also to the redefinition of the relation between the corporation and independent consultants.

From the point of view of income distribution, we can notice everywhere a net reduction in the number of household incomes situated between 70 percent and 190 percent of the median.[9] This numeric measurement criteria for the Fordist middle class has the advantage of showing how its compression has in fact been caused by downward mobility.

While this dynamic reflects the economic crisis of the Fordist middle class, it is not a sufficient explanation for its "positional" rearticulation, nor its distribution along the productive cycle. In the recovery cycle of the American economic cycle, the sectors which have created new jobs at the beginning of the 1990s as a response to the increase in consumption of the employed population were, in decreasing order: leisure and entertainment,[10] health services, information and technology, cable TV, research and consulting, nonprofit organizations and museums, education. In the majority of cases, these jobs are various forms of self-employment, small entrepreneurship and temporary positions, with all their negative aspects with respect to the length of the working day, job insecurity, and lack of benefits. This is the professional constellation of the post-Fordist middle class, which redefined itself in terms of income and professions, trying to capitalize on its own stock of knowledge and creativity. But this leaves the middle class at the mercy of market demand.

It would be a mistake to believe that the disappearance of the Fordist middle class (which can be measured with the classic criteria of income distribution around either the average or the median levels) coincides with the "proletarization of the middle-income brackets." It would also be a mistake to presuppose that the middle class behaves in a homogenous manner or that it shares the same goals, derived from its stable position within the economic-productive circuit. An analysis of the most recent electoral results shows that everywhere, rightward shifts reflect an extremely composite electoral base, where we find beside the small entrepreneur protesting tax rates, temporary workers, the unemployed, and perhaps most surprisingly, even a growing number of employees. The changing nature of political alliances stands in contrast to the party fidelity typical of the Fordist era, and it exposes not only the miserable aspect of instability, but also the loss of security deriving from the erosion of the protections offered by social institutions.

If it is true, as is commonly relayed in expressions such as "middle" or "working" class, that there is a group of people sharing some deep commonalities externally *signified* by a similarity in occupation, education and moral values, then the term of "class" as *simple rhetoric* is perfectly adequate to the newly born middle class. This is a *"rhetorical class,"* which identifies in the images and the clichés created for it; it is the product of a projection that allows for a feeling of belonging beyond all internal differences.

Using the term "middle class" is a social act and means to "enter in a relation with others," that is, to insert oneself in a "social transaction." This is a rhetorical-linguistic transaction, like all transactions traversing the entirety of the post-Fordist economic process. Language, communicative action through the images, symbols and signs of the middle class, in fact produces this very class, externalizing what is common to this "heterogeneous aggregation": the need for stability, security, tradition and identity.

In this case, more than ever, the *sign* of a value created *ex nihilo*—that is, on the basis of nothing at all—succeeds in producing power and consensus and realizes itself in a tangible form. But this would not be possible if communication were not already the foundation of the economic-productive process, integral to its very nature and functioning. If this were not the case, we would not need to belong to the middle class, to feel "superior" to the lower social strata and an integral part of the "working, useful, productive class" deserving an adequate political representation.

The mass conversion to neoliberal ideology, which paradoxically makes of individualism a collective value producing a feeling of supra-personal belonging, is not mysterious at all. Nor should we simply decry it. What counts is not that unbridled individualism, with its *mors tua vita mea* morality, is hardly compatible with the desire to belong to a social class. The important thing is that this desire to belong exists, and that it is just as strong as the real experience of collective disaggregation.

The rhetoric of the middle class, of course, today produces this sense of belonging only through publicity: the public sphere is only the upended image of a political community that in reality does not exist. However, it is from the need for community that we need to overturn the commercialized rhetoric of the political language of community. The problem raised by the middle class is not that of overcoming or transgressing its self-image, but of managing to stay with it, to in-sist and re-sist within it, deepening this experience until we can let "its origin shine" and touch its needs with our own hands.[11] The political critique of middle class expectations and desires, and of their betrayal at the hands of those who manipulate them for their own goals, should not let us forget the productive power of language, of the rhetoric defining values and desires. The struggle is situated within language, in the ability to produce other versions of the same fundamental desire of belonging to a community. The real problem is how to create other *common places* able to fill the gap between the desire for community and its internal, *political* inconsistencies.

3. State and Market

The diffusion of the post-Fordist paradigm in an increasingly globalized economic context forces us to rethink the relation between State and market.

First of all, in the new economy the reversal of the relation between production and consumption imposes a redefinition of Say's Law: it is no longer the offer that creates its own demand, but the opposite. The centrality of demand in the determination of the times and modes of production forces us to "reverse our thinking" on all the relations of cause and effect typical of conventional economic theories.

We spoke already of the function of inventory: its presence is a sign of an excess in productive capacity with respect to actual demand, which leads to various interventions both on the work force and on the means of production responsible for the excess. The goal is to establish a real-time equilibrium between offer and demand. This equilibrium is threatened every time the market cannot absorb the entirety of the goods and services produced by the economy.

Say's law has the following peculiarity: it defines the quantitative relation between offer and demand in terms of equilibrium, where a certain quantity of needed goods corresponds to an identical quantity of produced goods. This relation, however, has always posed a real problem, because in a market economy it can only be expressed in *monetary* terms. In the original version of Say's law, this means that the offer can create an identical demand only because *monetary incomes* allow the purchase of the entirety of produced goods.

This is easily said, but terribly difficult to verify in reality. The obsession of all capitalists is always to *sell* one's products, because without sales, goods simply become excessive inventory. Only the sale can realize a *monetary* profit. At most, the excessive inventory—which at that point in the capitalist's books figures not in the sales column, but in the costs column—will eventually be sold at a much lower price. In any case, this has always been a real problem, which economists solved by *assuming* that Say's equation is in fact true, that is, that the monetary values of offer and demand are in fact identical.

There is no need to go over the debate on the validity of Say's law, whether it is only "partially true," since the presence of money poses the risk of breaking the exchange chain (in fact, those who have sold might not buy again, interrupting the concatenation of the exchange actions), or in fact "completely false," since the monetary incomes directly generated by the economic system are structurally insufficient to absorb the volume of offered merchandises.

For our discussion, it will suffice to say that the welfare state has in fact greatly helped capitalist growth, if only through its role in redistributing income toward the less affluent classes (which have a high propensity for consumption) and in acquiring goods and services from the private sector. Since the 1929 crisis, the welfare State was in fact a "vehicle" for mass consumption. Without it, it would have been difficult, if not downright impossible, to generalize the Fordist paradigm, which succeeded in insuring the correspondence between mass production and mass consumption. The increase in nominal income auspicated by Ford in order to sell his cars would not have been enough; the State needed to intervene with its *added* demand, on top of what was generated within the private sphere. And in fact, in the Fordist economy the salary has always been considered both as a cost and as a decisive income fundamental to insuring the continuity of production.

It would seem, then, that corporate techniques of production and organization typical of just-in-time have allowed us to eliminate, at least in part, the grave problem of the equilibrium between offer and demand. Precisely because in this new productive system excessive inventory has become an *indicator* of imbalances between offer and demand, the structuring of the productive process on the basis of the zero-stock principle succeeds in avoiding the classical risks of an overproduction crisis.

From the point of view of the producer-seller of goods and services, this means that a salary today represents mostly a cost, and no longer as an expense. For the producer-seller, what really counts is the short-term response to the variations in demand, because for him the demand is data to which he will tailor his offer. It doesn't matter that much that this demand is also the result of the salary given to his own workers; what matters is that the prices of his merchandises are such that they will insure the sale of all that he produces in real time. The post-Fordist producer does not produce *for* a future demand, but *from* an already existing demand. The variable of time, with the tendential reduction to zero from the act of production to the act of consumption (the coming together of the ex ante and the ex post), clouds the perception of salary as income, while reinforcing the one that sees it as a cost to be reduced to the minimum in order to stay competitive.

This is why the welfare State, both as a fiscal mechanism for income redistribution and as a generator of salary income, cannot but represent an obstacle for the post-Fordist capitalist. On the one hand the State is perceived as the cause for the excessive cost of labor (in terms of taxes and benefits), and on the other it is at the source of high borrowing costs when it raises the interest rates in order to shift savings toward the public debt. From the point of view of *monetary incomes*, the real-time equilibrium between offer and demand will be reached through the participation of the salaried employees in the company's profits, and therefore only *after* the actual sale of its products.

It is from this perspective that in the post-Fordist regime credit is increasingly directed toward consumption, and not production: consumer credit, in its most different forms (leasing, installment plans, small credit, credit cards of all sorts), allows to anticipate that part of the salary that the company can no longer prepay on the account of future demand. Consumer credit has taken the role that belonged to the welfare State in the Fordist regime, insofar as it allows for an actual, *monetary*, demand able to buy the entirety of what is produced. The traditional role of the welfare State as ultimate guarantor of effective demand is being privatized: the bank system is better equipped for insuring a demand focused on the actual consumers who, if they still don't have the income to buy what they want, can receive the difference, directly or indirectly, from the bank.

The just-in-time production system feeds on the atomization of a market where the taste and the readiness to buy on the part of consumers is decisive and needs to be known, explored and immediately satisfied as soon as it arises. The relation between sale outlets and the bank system becomes extremely tight: this is why banks develop a whole array of payment systems aimed at smoothing and facilitating the realization of the equilibrium between offer and demand. The result is that not only is the welfare State progressively losing its legitimacy, but also that salaried workers are more and more dependent on a credit system that forces them to immediately translate into monetary income any increase in productivity: this creates a labor trap even more than it does a consumerist one. The idea of distributing work positions on the basis of productivity gains in order to combat unemployment clashes with "consumer fever," even if post-Fordist "consumerism" is in fact a *coercion to work* just so that people "can repay their debt."

The globalization of the economy adds another element to the delegitimizing of the State's economic role. In a globalized system, State investments do not guarantee the "multiplying effects" dear to Fordist economic theories. Building a road, a public school or anything else no longer necessarily means creating jobs in one's own country (be it the nation, a region or any other administrative entity).

The income created in the process might end up somewhere else, precisely because the deregulation of the global economies implicitly opened all borders. "In today's global economy, putting money in the consumer's pockets might mean sending it abroad, with no benefits for the national economy."[12] A Swiss citizen, when he or she buys a new television or a compact disk, is in fact sending Swiss francs to Japan, Korea or any other country. As the economy becomes more globalized, the nation's role shrinks, vanifying all efforts to combat unemployment with traditional anti-cyclical measures. The terrain of the struggle against unemployment is disappearing as an actual space of income production through public investment.

In order to be effective in its struggle against unemployment, the State's strategies are becoming less dependent on the distribution of actual wealth, and more dependent on the distribution of knowledge, on the ability to exploit available resources. While in the post-Fordist regime the role of the State is actually becoming less prominent as a distributor of income, it does acquire a strategic importance as a purveyor of immaterial abilities founded on knowledge and on the valorization of the individual (or of a certain geographical region) within the global market.

Today, we know full well that unemployment can't be beaten without a substantial redefinition of requalification programs and that poverty has to be confronted with well-planned redistribution measures. Why, then, we may ask, does any reasonable proposal of this kind regularly clash with the State's budgetary limits before even confronting the neoliberal programs of fiscal reduction?

The fact is that public finances are still adopting a Fordist kind of accounting instrument, insofar as investment expenses still play an absurdly bigger role than does the managing of the current budget. This very repartition represents a very important political-economical obstacle. It is on its basis that investment expenses drain away resources from current budgetary expenses, or at least greatly impede their increase. This is caused by the zealous will to finance investment expenses (equipment, machinery, buildings, civil engineering projects, etc.).

It is true that material goods are depreciating even more quickly. One can understand the pursuit of a financing policy in order to avoid leaving excessive debt to the future generations. However, it is incomprehensible that on this basis any struggle against unemployment or poverty should be nipped in the bud.

Currently, many items are accounted for as current expenses (let's just think about education), but in fact they are investments that future generations desperately need. Still, in current forms of accounting they are listed as expenses and, most importantly, as expenses that need to be reduced if political authorities decide to increase their investments in material goods and in their financing. In an economy where hardware is progressively losing its importance with respect to software, it is completely illogical (except in terms of corruption) to keep reasoning as if future generations should inherit from us quickly obsolescent structures rather than the knowledge, cultural environment and social cohesion adequate for the new economy.

We can no longer calculate financing on the basis of the depreciation time of real estate structures. Likewise, we can't use yearly maintenance expenses or salary obligations as an excuse for not investing in immaterial goods at a higher level than what is left of the difference between fiscal revenues, investments and financing. If it is possible for a single individual to incur a debt for his or her own education—a debt that will be gradually paid back over one's professional career—then it is not clear why the same reasoning should not be applied to the educational or even redistributive plans that could benefit the collectivity.

It is not surprising that the space left empty by the State's lack of initiative is being filled by private projects in various sectors previously considered to be public, such as education. In fact, there is an abundance of capital for several reasons: the savings imposed and managed by institutional investors (such as pension plans) have increased disproportionally; the investments in former socialist economies have remained modest; and last but not least, fixed capital investments are increasingly inconsistent while investments of money and capital in immaterial activities is becoming more significant.

The abundance of capital should allow us to deemphasize the role that the State attributes to interest rates in determining public debt. According to traditional theories, as debt and negative interests increase, there would be a decrease in available financial resources. In fact, however, this is no longer true in an era when the recoveries themselves are not inflationary because of globalization phenomena and stagnant salary rates.

The role played in the State's budgetary decisions by investments in infrastructures, fixed capital and financing is not easily understandable from an analytical point of view, unless, of course, it is under the aegis of corruption. The largest part of these investments normally concerns the *territory* as a whole, so that while it is true that the high rates of financing quickly eliminate the debts contracted by the State (for instance, in the construction of a road or of a railway line), it is also true that they don't take into consideration the depreciation time of the realized works, which normally are longer than the financing plan. It is certainly true that in this way public debt is quickly reduced, but nobody talks about the *occultation* of the capital that remains after the elimination of debt: as an example, a railway line keeps functioning long *after* having been entirely financed, becoming a publicly-owned asset.

The occultation of the State's—that is, of the collectivity's—property, which is the consequence of the gap between the rate of financing and the rate of depreciation of material goods, allows the State to keep its policies of withdrawing resources from current expenses (which normally are distributed incomes) while at the same time creating all the conditions for fiscal reductions. The neoliberal right, in fact, start crusading against fiscal pressures as soon as they see a public debt reduction. Neoliberal pressures get stronger when fiscal revenues are high, even when they increase not as a consequence of an increase in tax rates, but *of revenues*. This is how the possibility of intervening on the income distribution front is doubly reduced: we have higher financing rates accompanied by decreased fiscal pressure (defined both in absolute *and* relative terms, with respect to profit margins).

This "paleocapitalistic" accounting approach keeps the debate about "more or less State" on a totally unproductive level that forces the administration to behave like a private corporation. It is paradoxical that while the most advanced entrepreneurial sectors have recognized the strategic role of intellectual capital and do all they can to develop adequate techniques of corporate accounting, the State should stick to the logic of small and medium enterprises. These are the companies that in order to finance their investments need to speculate most on their dependents' labor, that increasingly rely on outsourcing practices, reducing their maintenance expenses to a minimum and polluting the environment just to save money, and creating *negative externalities* that become the responsibility of the collectivity.

We should also remark that the land, the territory, has played a fundamental role in the United States during the Reagan years. In the 1980s, neoliberal policies have legitimized the wildest real estate speculations, causing the saving institutions for the low and middle classes (the Savings and Loans Associations) that had been completely deregulated to invest in the real estate market according to a corrupt logic benefiting both Republican *and* Democratic politicians. According to the American economist James O'Connor:

> In the 1980s, one of the secrets of the economic boom was the increase in consumer demand determined by the expansion of mortgage and consumer financing in relation to the consumers' income. This was caused by the structural shift from manufacturing to the exploitation of environmental resources and finance.[13]

In fact, the real estate, construction and financing sectors have created their own demand only to respond to it by offering cheap money, thereby raiding the savings of middle- and lower-class consumers. The final result of these operations is a long series of bank defaults. The State then had to cover the debts of the savings institutions, an operation that effectively withdrew (and will continue to withdraw) redistributable income from the most impoverished social populations. In Europe, the policies aimed towards a reduction of welfare costs are now following the same Reagan-inspired logic ten years after the fact. At the core of this argument, however, we still find the territory, the space where political alliances are born out of the possibility of a private takeover of national collective assets.

The reality is that the unwillingness to focus the State's strategies on the real issues created by the new post-Fordist economy has created a political block favoring neoliberal policies. Entrepreneurs, private consultants, temporary workers and those dependent employees always under the threat of layoffs can't see any reason to support a welfare state whose privileges (job security and pension guarantees) are much more visible than its role in supporting the community. The State's intentions are of little consequence: the only thing that matters is that this corporatist view is able to assemble an anti-statist middle class that is easily manipulated by rightist arguments.

It is difficult, if not impossible, to find a way out of this impasse without a political mobilization of communicative-relational activities, immaterial labor and intellectual capital. It is hard to oppose neoliberal trends without developing the political strategies of the "cognitariat." The problem is not to "conquer the center," running after the rhetorical myth of the middle class and adapting one's language and political program to neoliberal "commonplaces." These commonplaces have a material foundation, they reflect an actual social and political composition, and owe their political strength to our inability to think the relation between State and market in different terms.

The current resentment against the State originates from the failed political recognition of the new productive classes, and from the lack of public support for the relational-communicative abilities that private capital is currently exploiting *without paying for them*.[14] Capital uses competition to reward productivity (we can think of the small companies, or the independent contractors that outbid each other trying to obtain a contract), but the logistical effort, the utilization of cognitive abilities, the hours and experience mobilized to realize the work—without even talking about the investment in professional training—are not included in the bid, for fear of losing the contract. We are actually witnessing a kind of self-exploitation on the part of the "middle class" that can become a hatred against a State which is not where it should be (offering free training classes, essential at this level of professional skill, or covering the new risks associated with the post-Fordist mode of production), while it is always present as a fiscal entity. But the definition of taxable income has become increasingly abstract, as it does not take into consideration the expenses necessary to be competitive on today's job market.

4. Towards an Extraterritorial State

The historic dilemma confronting today's State, squeezed between the neoliberal right and the accounting logic inherited from the Fordist era, is nonetheless opening new spaces for political action.

These spaces are at the intersection of the gradual *transformation of politics into administration* and the growing role of *civil society* in confronting some of the most acute and emblematic problems of post-Fordist societies, such as structural unemployment, drugs, the AIDS epidemic and the situation of immigrants and refugees.

The post-Fordist regime entails the crisis of the classic institutions typical of representative democracies, and even more so, of the parliamentary system. This crisis originates in the overlap between productive and communicative action, which has fractured the classic separation between economical and political spheres while con-*fusing* instrumental and politico-communicative activities. This has unleashed social and political processes that are not understandable through classical political rationality.

The first consequence of this crisis is the proliferation of parties and movements that present themselves as representing the collectivity on the basis of *limited* interests and "themes," as can be seen in the increasing difficulty on the part of the Executive and Legislative powers to create a consensus around issues of common interest. What we call *Berlusconism* is not merely an Italian phenomenon due to an "informal golpe," as Paul Virilio defined it. It is simply the earliest expression of an interest-based political action within the communicative sector. *Berlusconism* is not a "television anomaly" that can be liquidated with some kind of antitrust law, but is in fact an experiment in post-Fordist governance. In it, we find the explosive synthesis of all the traits of the historical trend unleashed by the post-Fordist shift.

If anything, Berlusconi's victory signifies the inability, on the part of his opponents, to understand the deeper meaning of the current transformations and thus respond to them by radically innovating upon the current paradigms of political action. If the left wants to become relevant again in its attempts to counter the perversions of neoliberism, it would be much more productive to try and identify, behind *and* within the political-media system of *Berlusconism*, the real social forces on which it rests.

Communicative technologies are not instruments of exile from the world, nor reversible deviations from reality. Rather, they are mechanisms contributing to *the construction of the world* that we experience as a society, in our way of *being together*. If in Berlusconism "being together," living in the *public sphere*, means to be within the world of *publicity*—and this is one of its most hateful aspects—then what we need is another way of being together. What we need is *another language*, able to produce the public sphere as *political community*.

At any rate, post-Fordist parliamentary democracies have appeared incapable from the very beginning of facing the problems of post-Fordist societies, but through the adoption of antisocial measures. Once it conquers power, the entrepreneurial class (which in Italy, with Berlusconi, represents the interests of both the communication and the financial-real estate sectors) soon betrays its own inadequacy to tackle complex problems. The technologies of just-in-time that they would like to introduce into public administration in order to "rationalize" democratic institutions, interpret the demands of the citizens (which is determined through polls) as an effective demand coming from one people, one universe, while in fact the very logic of the "political market" should tell us that we are dealing with the demands of a multitude of subjects, of a pluriverse. The polling system is the equivalent of the mechanisms devised to collect consumer information at the moment of the sale. It freezes in the moment a cross section of civil society, creating a "public opinion" that remains abstract from time and space.

The immense speed of information technologies, which disintegrates space and any concrete territory, any reality rooted in history and in the effective encounter between individual and collectivity, cannot suppress the slow, stubborn and heavy reality that constitutes our daily lives.[15] The technical death of Time in post-Fordist societies is contradicted by lived time, which remains concrete and slow and still shapes the social lives and lived experiences of the citizens inhabiting a real territory. As the old adage says: "Only the lightly armed can march quickly." Slow time is the "perfect time" of the Chinese tale told by Calvino in his American lecture on quickness: "At the end of these ten years, Chuang-tzu took up his brush and, in an instant, with a single stroke, he drew a crab, the most perfect crab ever seen."

In fact, in postmodern societies democracy is always situated between *the time of communication* and the *space of social relations*. It is in this space in between that the most different versions of the immanent conflict of modernity occur, between the One and the multiple, the individual and the collectivity, the general and the contingent, the particular and the universal, between direct democracy and representative democracy, between the State and civil society.

We talk more and more about a "modest," "subsidiary," "inciting," or "supervising" kind of State, precisely because these expressions emphasize a new—more fluid and complex—articulation of the relations between State and civil society. The transformation in the State's agency is perhaps more visible in the relation between the communication of its goals and their realization. These silent mutations can be observed most clearly in the political measures that aim at the most extreme forms of social marginality, such as the problem of drug addiction and the social conflicts that make it explode on the urban scene. The need to know from the inside the dynamics of the drug market, its territorial logic, and the most diverse behaviors of the marginal populations involved in it, forces the State to ask civil society to engage in the elaboration of measures both of prevention and reinsertion. The "drug problem," because of its dramatic urgency, becomes a "technical" problem that public administrations have to face on the terrain itself, without the "obstacles" created by parliamentary debates: the drug addict strays from the rules of consensual and "discursive" democracy, and to consider him as a citizen would be contradictory in terms of representative democracy. The drug-addict is incapable of representing the whole of civil society: he is, in fact, a marginal, he is not included in a representative democracy whose rules he does not abide by, he is an "impossible subject," irreducible to the norms of common living. As such, he can only be considered an "administrative subject," outside of the democratic debate on the deeper causes of his existence.[16]

The "inciting" State, which appeals to civil society, remains in any case a "poor" State that imposes strict conditions on the disbursement of the *seed money* needed by the different organizations in their efforts to elaborate concrete intervention projects.[17] The accounting logic of the State is thereby passed on to civil society, and the constraints accompanying public monies often prevent them from innovating upon the work performed by State-employed operators. The social workers from the nongovernmental associations, in addition to the knowledge that they have acquired in close contact with the drug addicts, often appear more credible precisely because they are not representatives of the State. But these kinds of *post facto* decentralized intervention risks can become another way to assert State control on civil society due to the rules accompanying the distribution of funds. Furthermore, these associations don't possess the prerogatives of the State, insofar as their operators cannot benefit from the possibility to open a space for democratic debate about the resistance that they face in the field.

In fact, the true problem is the definition of the place of intervention for the associations summoned into action precisely where the State cannot go. It is on the local scale that they are positioned, because it is on this plane that we find the most problematic subjects. However, this is also the place where we again encounter the question of democracy, which apparently had been liquidated through a purely technical approach to the issue of drug addiction. Common spaces such as the neighborhoods or other local entities are far from representing an ideal dimension where civil society could redefine its democratic criteria. And still, such criteria are necessary if we want the cooperation of a population that, however "sensitive" to the problem of drug addiction it may be, clearly prefers not to confront it in its own neighborhood. It is on the local level that the most urgent policies often stall because of residents rebelling against the opening of centers for controlled heroin distribution or AIDS prevention.

The local terrain is the place where we still find a feudal type of power structure functioning according to a microphysics of control that easily reaches the levels of "turf wars." Locally implemented services often collide with an abstract imaginary (according to which the drug-addict would be "young, criminal, HIV-positive" and so on) projected by the residents on all marginal subjects even before they become "clients" benefiting from these services. This happens with all those subjects whose reproduction depends on *spatial* practices (such as a street corner, an occupied building or a particular watering hole) that clash with the defensive strategies of the mainstream local population. These strategies of territorial defense in fact prevent decentralized public action within the civil society from being *effective*. And if the local policies adopted to confront issues that in fact involve society as a whole fail in their implementation, this becomes the failure of all social policies.

The clash between the involvement of civil society and the defense of the local territory forces us to redefine political initiative and decision-making processes. Public initiative is *powerless* when it founds its legitimacy on local grounds, because localism as such is a mix of material interests that prevent the applicability of initiatives aimed at solving dramatic problems that concern society *as a whole*. Localism territorializes social issues rooted in increasingly deterritorialized processes, such as the restructuration/immateriality of the productive processes and economic globalization with their destructuring consequences for poor countries and the ethnic wars reflecting the need for cultural identity on the wane of the Nation/State. It is true that we have to act locally, but the local particularizes issues of general interest.

We have talked at length about public measures against drug addiction (though in fact the same would apply to the new immigration issue) not because we want to overdramatize the limits of representative democracy and the attempts to overcome them by making politics a simple matter of administration. The fact is that these problems are very urgent since, in their absolute tangibility, they reflect much larger issues, particularly the role of civil society in redefining democracy.

Historically, the Right has always benefited from these "aporias," in these logical difficulties inherent to the functioning of representative democracies. Its racist hatred for any marginal existence is only the prologue to an authoritarian form of post-representative democracy, a democracy "without rights" that can only work by eliminating any form of resistance hindering the administrative *just-in-time*. For the Right, the drug addict, the refugee, the unemployed are the "human material" on which to experiment with the new technologies of social control, exactly as it happened when women, children and vagrants were shut off in workhouses and hospices during the first industrial revolution as the guinea pigs for the testing of the new industrial machinery, while also representing the synthesis of the economic-productive strength and the politico-disciplinary organization of the emerging powers.

The coercion exerted on the "excess population" created by the occupational crisis of an increasingly efficient industrial sector and the demographic explosion of the Southern countries is the true restoration program of the Right's "totalitarian democracy." The marginalized, comprised of uprooted, deterritorialized individuals deprived of their memories and traditions, constitute the human material on which the new Panopticon can be built. This will be a confining mechanism allowing for the daily, molecular and consistent exertion of Power's control to be internalized by the citizens. The "people" and their fear of any "different" form of life are in fact being *trained* by power on their own terrain, in the local space that they inhabit.

The mass of the "new poor" is one that can better work as guinea pigs for the new technologies of discipline and control underlying the totalitarian democracies of the future. They don't have a tradition that can be defended, they can't resist the salary blackmail, they are constantly confronted with the fear of falling back into the limbo of urban ghettos, into the misery of "smack," into the humiliation of public assistance. The poor don't protest, and they are often the last to find out that there has been a change in the ability, on the part of society, to alleviate human suffering in a non-repressive way.

In post-Fordist societies, the technologies of discipline and control all deal with space, with territories, because the growing immateriality of labor needs disciplinary mechanisms capable of normalizing the active population along spatial lines. The "new factory" is no longer conceived on the model of the workhouses or hospices of the early 1800s, but that of the streets and neighborhoods where the new social outcasts reside. The technologies of immaterial labor are experimenting with their ability to prevent the poor's revolt and insubordination in the urban space. These are media technologies, distributed according to a military logic of territorial control in order to monitor the movements of the most "dangerous individuals." Urban space is thus segmented in such a way that new residential areas will emerge from a growing process of spatial *apartheid*.[18]

Marginal populations are the guinea pigs for the planning implemented by Power on urban space, although what people who today feel safe don't know is that they could become subject to the same destiny one day. The exclusion suffered by drug addicts is planned, and all the more so considering how drug consumption traverses "normal" society, reaching into the most respectable professions. Similarly, the underlying racism of sedentary populations is simply the fear of recognizing *oneself* in the other, with a future marked by the uprooting and identity loss caused by the deterritorialization of productive processes. As livable space gets smaller as a consequence of the segmentation of space enacted in order to exclude the always changing "subjects at risk," the existential condition of the migrant is in fact generalized to apply to the entire population. Today's racism reflects the resentment toward a condition that belongs *to us all*, but one that we don't want to admit as such: this is why we attribute it to the other.

This is why we have to seriously analyze the problems created by the public measures imposed on the more marginalized groups of today's society. The conflict between public measures, civil society and localism surpasses the "controlled distribution of psychotropic substances" or the opening of refugees centers. What is at stake here is the political form of post-representative democracy, a form that the Right would like to organize around the spatial exclusion of marginal populations: this is the first step toward the "democracy without rights" that will soon be ours, and maybe without our being able to understand it.

We need to stand firm on the social and political rights of marginalized populations, and their problems should not be subject to purely technical interventions just to avoid a clash with conservative forces. Their rights of today will be our own rights of tomorrow. If the concrete interventions on behalf of the amelioration of their condition are met with local revolts, then we have to free ourselves from the trap of the territorial definition of citizenship. Territoriality, be it at the level of the nation, the city or the neighborhood, can no longer be the dimension that determines the definition of citizenship, not only because the global economy is, in fact, deterritorialized, but mostly because territoriality establishes interdictions, limits, borders and barriers that undermine the very notion of democracy.

"Nation-State means a State that makes of birth (that is, of naked life) the foundation of its own sovereignty."[19] Etymologically, "native" simply refers to birth, but the conservative defense of the territory has brought us to conflate the rights of men with those of a territorially defined citizen. The ambiguity of the expression "nation-state" consists in translating the rights of men into the rights of citizens while attributing to citizenship a territorial origin. This is how the territory where the citizens live allows us to free the notion of citizenship from its *biological* foundation. But the rights of men represent the original inscription of naked, natural life into the juridical-political order of the Nation-State.

In order to protect democracy from a regime that is actually plotting against it, we need to explore new forms of citizenship and new levels of representation. The extraterritorial State, a State that would ensure an equal representation for the multiple subjects constituting our social and civic space, is the dimension that we are now creating, precisely from the experience acquired within the local struggle against the biologic destruction caused by drug addiction.

In several Swiss cities (Geneva and Basel), the clashes between social workers and neighborhood residents caused by the opening of centers for the controlled distribution of drugs have resulted in the institution of a mediation space (*drogenstammtish*) aimed at bringing together the different parties involved in the dispute, addicts included. This was done in order to find mediation based on their lived experience, their knowledge and their respective interpretations of the rules necessary to the realization of concrete solutions. The "urban compromise" emerging from these early experiences is to be seen from an extraterritorial plane, because this is the only plane able to represent—according to the rules imposed by the State's laws—the plurality of languages expressing the subjects' desire to save their own lives.

This is only the first stage in the creation of an "extraterritorial State," but what makes these experiences interesting (even in their experimental form) is the fact that they originate in the concrete problem of preserving human life, and that on this basis they try to define the foundation of citizenship in a new way. The concrete nature of this initiative is not immediately (that is, in an un-mediated form) derived from its territorial implementation; on the very contrary: it is the result of a project elaborated by a multiplicity of actors representing themselves in their effort to realize it. It is the immaterial, the extraterritorial plane on which the project is discussed that defines the space of aggregation for the people involved in it. If we wanted to start from the materiality of the things that need to be done, involving different groups and associations only in a technical-instrumental way, we would simply cause a gang war (as happened with the Letten initiative in Zurich). There are no concrete solutions without politics, without institutional rules allowing us to draft the agreements necessary for opening a prevention service or any other social implement.

The notion of extraterritorial State emerging from these concrete experiences goes far beyond their specificity, and we can articulate it as follows:

1) *What* we are talking about is always *people's lives*, that is, the biological definition of our being-in-the-world. Therefore, we always start from an *eco*-logical matrix, in the literal sense of a discourse about the "home," about how to best organize humanity's abode.

2) What we *need* are *projects* bringing together subjects that define themselves precisely starting from these projects. In post-Fordist societies, political representation originates in the concrete projects that we want to realize. Representation is fleshed out in the immaterial vision, in the image of possible solutions. This is the exact opposite of the current regime, where political representation precedes the elaboration of projects that in this way are conditioned *ex ante* by the kind of party coalitions that are formed by the government. This political model is no longer adequate for solving the problems of post-Fordist societies because its founding mechanism is tied to political interests that might even be more *territorial* than they are class or interest based. The end of this political model also means the end of the distinction between Right and Left. But this distinction can still be measured *on the projects* that need to be realized to protect the life-conditions of society's members. Right and Left cannot be defined *a priori* as alternating poles: this amounts to reproducing in a different form the same party system that

has been incapable of solving the fundamental problems of post-Fordist societies.

3) The crisis of representation is the starting point for the construction of spaces for the mediation and interpretation of the rules allowing the realization of concrete projects regarding social life. These spaces are located between the general and the particular, between the sphere of fundamental rights and the actual living spaces of women and men. Civil society is then redefined on the basis of its different associations. The associations active in the field are no longer defined in instrumental terms, because the definition of the problems needing to be addressed can't simply be technical, but juridical, political and institutional. The associations of civil society, the knowledge that they have accumulated, contribute to the definition of the "social machine" enabling the living labor of its citizens.

4) The *communication* among different subjects, precisely as diversity invests with ever-growing intensity our *deepest experiences*, cannot be only linguistic in nature, in the oral and written forms inherited from the "discursive democracy" theorized by Habermas. The languages used by the different actors in the realization of their projects have to be multiple if we want them to express their thought and their experiences in an effective manner. The most recent information technologies allow us to think human communication in freer terms. The new technologies are evolving toward a communication model based on the figurative representation of mental models. The communication through animated images in interactive technologies should not be considered a technical application, but as an example of the different human languages that coexist with the spoken and written language of the juridical

State founded on "discursive democracy." Communication problems are linguistic only when language helps us toward the social con-division of what is to be done. A better integration is created by the coexistence of different languages, because integration problems cannot be solved linguistically, but only by taking language as an instrument for *producing* people's interiority.

The plurality and freedom of languages is the preliminary condition for social life, but as such it is the instrument for elaborating the rules for instituting spaces of coexistence. The institutional nature of language is strengthened by expanding its field of action to a plurality of subjects who, when they are free to express themselves in their own terms, can "in-form" their interiority.

This is the embryonic form of a democracy conceived as a variable geometry, because all compromises will be partial, as the result of successive struggles and negotiations. But the very essence of democracy is to put conflicts to work, creating the conditions for the emergence of different experiences and for the creation of spaces where a reasonable mediation among local rationalities can be achieved. What is reasonable is not the intolerant repression of the conflicts originating in different subjective logics, because these logics are society's flesh and blood, and in fact represent its wealth. What is reasonable is allowing these different logics to come out into the open, to express themselves on an equal plane without losing their specificity, and to create struggles and confrontations that will lead us towards more equitable ways of living together. What is reasonable is to see the "sock drawer" as a place for friendship and love.

Afterword to the Italian Edition

In the last few years, the questions raised by this book—originally published in Switzerland in 1994—have been studied, discussed and criticized by others with the rigor that they deserved. Today we have a plethora of studies about post-Fordism as a form of production. But what has remained problematic even in the wealth of current reflections is the ability to think through the connection between the general transformation of economic organization and today's political forms of government. I believe that one of the reasons for this difficulty is to be found precisely in the overlapping of production and communication, in the "linguistic turn" of the economy that already in the 1980s appeared as evident as it was innovative to anyone interested in the sociological consequences of our new way of working. The fact is that language is no joke, particularly when it becomes an immediately productive force. And in fact, in the 1990s the distance between the linguistic machine and the war apparatus emerged as much less than we had imagined.

The advent of language in the productive sphere has immediate consequences on economic indicators, in their role as measuring units for the capitalist command over processes of valorization. Power is increasingly defined as command over the forms of life, over the concrete body of the social community. When we put to work communication and intersubjective relations we put to work feelings and emotions, and finally the entire life of the people. In the 1990s, suffering, pain and humiliation experienced in the work place has constituted the hostile objectives of neoliberalism. The real paradigmatic shift, however, resides in the forms of command, in the articulations of power, because there is nothing particularly new in language-as-work.

This is why I thought it necessary to study the monetary and financial articulations of the post-Fordist economy. In my book *Il Denaro va: Esodo e rivoluzione dei mercati finanziari*,[1] published in 1998, I tried to emphasize the new financial economy that invests the domestic lives of common families. I saw in the movement toward the placement of domestic savings in the stock market the premises for the Asian, Brazilian and Russian crises. It might seem strange, but in fact it is precisely capital's ability to avoid a truly planetary crisis that allows us to explain its reliance on war. If we want to produce capital through life, we need to remember how little life is worth in the eyes of power.

— April 1999

Notes

Introduction

1. In 1980—twenty years earlier—Christian Marazzi and Sylvere Lotringer edited a special issue of Semiotext(e), *Autonomia: Post-Political Politics*, meant to publicize the plight of Autonomist intellectuals and activists who had just been being jailed or displaced by state repression in Italy.

2. My translation of chapter II of *Capital and Affects* was published in a special issue on "Italian Post-Workerist Thought" (*Substance*, 112, v. 36, n. 1, 2007). Both *Capital and Language: From the New Economy to the War Economy* (2002) and *The Violence of Financial Capitalism*, were published by Semiotext(e) in 2008.

3. A good example would be the mysterious drop in the Dow Jones index on May 6, 2010, which has been widely attributed to a human error amplified by international computer networks.

4. Franco "Bifo" Berardi, *The Soul at Work: From Alienation to Autonomy*, trans. Francesca Cadel and Giuseppina Mecchia, Los Angeles: Semiotext(e), 2009, 192.

5. Gilles Deleuze and Félix Guattari, *What Is Philosophy?*, New York: Columbia University Press, 1994, 12.

6. Christian Marazzi, *Il comunismo del capitale: finanziariazzione, biopolitiche del lavoro e crisi globale*, Verona: Ombre Corte, 2010, 24–25. Forthcoming, Semiotext(e), 2012.

Prologue

1. [In English in the original. Trans.]

1. Starting from Work

1. [Marazzi here is talking about the recession of 1992 that marked the end of George H.W. Bush's presidency. Trans.]

2. John Maynard Keynes, *The General Theory of Employment, Interest and Money* (New York: Harcourt Brace, 1936b), 313–314.

3. For a detailed analysis of the socioeconomic transformation in Switzerland tied to the concept of lean production, see Sergio Agustoni, Christian Marazzi, Bruno Strozzi, *La Svizzera verso un deserto industriale? Ristrutturazioni aziendali, lavoro autonomo e tempo di lavoro* (Como: Nodolibri, 1995).

4. See Peter Drucker, *Postcapitalist Society* (New York: Harper Collins, 1993), 72–74. One can also consult Federico Butera, *Il castello e la rete: Impresa, organizzazioni e professioni nell'Europa degli anni '90* (Milano: Angeli, 1991). On issues related to the outsourcing of production and independent consulting, it is important to read Sergio Bologna's works, such as "Problemi del lavoro autonomo in Italia" (II), *Altreregioni*, 2/93.

5. The first agreement concerning barcodes in the United States dates back to April 3, 1973.

6. See Alvin Toffler, *Powershift: Knowledge, Wealth and Violence at the Edge of the 21st Century* (New York: Bantam Books, 1990). We particularly recommend reading the first three sections of the book.

7. See, by Benjamin Coriat, *Penser à l'envers* (Paris: Christian Bourgeois, 1991). By the same author, one should consult "Ohno et l'école japonaise de gestion de production: un point de vue d'ensemble," in Helena Sumiko Hirata, ed., *Autour du modèle japonais* (Paris: L'Harmattan, 1992). See also Giuseppe Bonazzi, "Qualità totale e produzione snella: la lezione giapponese presa sul serio," *Il Mulino*, 346 (1993). For an analysis and bibliography of the post-Fordist paradigm, see also Umberto Russi, "L'imagination au travail" (Mémoire de maîtrise en Sciences Sociales, Université de Lausanne, 1994).

8. See Paolo Virno, *Convenzione e materialismo: L'unicità senza aurea* (Rome: Theoria, 1986). By the same author, also see *Mondanità: L'idea di "mondo" tra esperienza sensibile e sfera pubblica* (Rome: Manifestolibri, 1994). These texts are essential to the analysis of the paradigmatic shift represented by post-Fordism.

9. [In English in the original. Trans.]

10. This seems to be one of the most important conclusions reached by Ronny Bianchi in her doctoral thesis, entitled *Le modèle industriel Italien; réflexion théorique et historique des années 80* (Université de Paris 13, September 1994).

11. See Robert Boyer and André Orléan, "Les transformations des conventions salariales entre théorie et histoire: D'Henry Ford au fordisme," in *Revue Economique* (March 1992, 2), 233–272.

12. See Massimo Cacciari, "All'origine del concetto di innovazione: Schumpeter e Weber," in *Pensiero negativo e razionalizzazione* (Marsilio: Venezia 1977).

13. See André Gorz, *Critique of Economic Reason* (London: Verso, 1989/2011) and also Zygmunt Bauman, *Memories of Class: The Pre-History and After-Life of Class* (London: Routledge, 1982).

14. See Virno, *Convenzione e materialismo*, 81–85.

15. See André Gorz, *Critique of Economic Reason.*

16. See Virno, *Convenzione e materialismo*, 81–85.

17. On the "Turing machine" as founding "principle" for new technologies, see Joseph Weizenbaum, *Computer Power and Human Reason: From Judgment to Calculation* (New York: Freeman, 1995).

18. In *La Machine Univers: Création, cognition et culture informatique* (Paris: La Découverte, 1987), Pierre Lévy devotes several pages to a comparison between the philosophy of language of Ludwig Wittgenstein and the one expressed by the founders of information technologies, such as Wiener and McCulloch. The essential difference is that the philosopher is still intrigued by the "ineffable" and its mystique, while the theoreticians of computer languages, while allowing for a proliferation of languages, stop whenever these languages cannot be translated in logical-formal structures. "The inventors of cybernetics conceived man as a logical automaton dealing with information. They stopped to what is sayable and, forgetting who they were, they neglected the ineffable that Wittgenstein had theorized" (129, our translation). The same conclusions, but on a purely linguistic basis, were reached by Roberta De Monticelli in *Dottrine dell'intelligenza: Saggio su Frege e Wittgenstein* (Bari: De Donato, 1981).

19. See Jürgen Habermas, *The Theory of Communicative Action. Reason and the Rationalization of Society* (London: Atheneum Press, 1986), and *The Philosophical Discourse of Modernity: Twelve Lectures* (Cambridge: MIT Press, 1998). A very useful publication is the volume edited by Marcello Ostinelli and Virginio Pedroni, *Fondazione e critica della comunicazione: Studi su Habermas* (Milan: Angeli, 1992).

20. Umberto Eco, *The Limits of Interpretation* (Bloomington: Indiana University Press, 1990), 5–6. It is strange that Eco felt he had the "duty" to impose "objective" limits to textual interpretation after having himself contributed—by his own admission—to their removal about thirty years ago, thereby legitimizing Derrida's theories. It is strange that this move coincided with the *crisis* of the limits of interpretation caused by communication's entry into production, a crisis that never appears in Eco's writings. His seems, on the contrary, the desperate attempt to keep within the Enlightenment framework endangered by the post-Fordist revolution. We don't question here *the need* to establish limits, but the sphere and the new terrain where they are being redefined or at least identified.

21. See Jacques Bidet, *Théorie de la modernité* (Paris: PUF, 1990), 96–118.

22. Gorz, in his *Critique of Economic Reason*, devotes an entire chapter to Habermas, and there his critique seems to hold water (see 212–20). But later in the same book, with regard to the issue of work in the reproductive sphere, he reintroduces Habermas in a prominent fashion, showing his limited understanding of the interpenetration between instrumental and communicative actions. This demonstrates once again, Habermas' power of attraction, which reappears as soon as critical analysis has to overcome the limits of traditional political categories.

23. On this issue, see Paolo Virno, "Il linguaggio in mezzo al guado," *Luogo commune*, II, n. 2 (1991), where he comments on Giorgio Agamben's thoughts about the non-naturality of inherited language (*Infanzia e storia* [Turin: Einaudi, 1978]) that was similar to the critique of Habermas articulated by Gorz. Actually, this position goes back to 1876 in the theories of the American linguist William D. Whitney, articulated in his *The Life and Growth of Language: An Outline of Linguistic Science*. Also see, by Agamben, the essay "La cosa stessa," in Gianfranco Dalmasso, ed., *Di-segno: La giustizia nel discorso* (Milan: Jaca Books, 1984): "The presupposing structure of language is the structure of tradition: in language we presuppose and trade (both in the literal and figurative sense) the thing itself, so that language may bear on something... The sinking of the thing itself can only be the foundation for the constitution of a tradition" (9). In economic terms, we would say that before transforming values into prices, we need to *produce* value, that is to "bring into being" the living, subjective work of men. This is the presupposition of the "traditional" form of wage labor. We are always dealing with the same issue of transformation, of our *going beyond* the form.

24. Umberto Galimberti, *Parole nomadi* (Milano: Feltrinelli, 1999), 99 [our translation].

25. This is the critique of Habermas formulated by Emanuele Severino in his book *La tendenza fondamentale del nostro tempo* (Milano: Adelphi, 1988), 89–109.

26. As quoted in Habermas, *Justification and Application: Remarks on Discourse Ethics* (Cambridge: MIT Press, 1993), 123.

27. [Here Marazzi is clearly referring to the Italian political and cultural situation during the early 1990s, when the Christian Democrats and the Socialists were being destroyed by legal prosecutions, and Berlusconi was becoming a prominent political figure after having made his fortune in the television broadcasting, publishing and advertising business. Trans.]

28. See Giorgio Gargani, *Stili di analisi: L'unità perduta del metodo filosofico* (Milan: Feltrinelli, 1993).

29. Martin Heidegger, *Elucidations of Hölderlin's Poetry* (Amherst: Humanity Books, 2000), 54–55.

30. See Marco Ravelli, "Con la fabbrica integrate l'addio al fordismo," *il manifesto* (July 3, 1994).

31. See Richard D. Freeman, ed., *Working under Different Rules* (New York: Russell Sage Foundation, 1994), 1–25.

32. George Akerlof, "Labor Contracts as Partial Gift Exchange," in George Akerlof, ed., *An Economic Theorist's Book of Tales: Essays that Entertain the Consequences of New Assumptions in Economic Theory* (Cambridge: Cambridge University Press, 1984), 145–174.

33. Ruth Benedict, *The Chrysanthemum and the Sword: Patterns of Japanese Culture* (Boston: Houghton Mifflin, 1946).

34. As quoted in Richard Swedberg, *Economics and Sociology* (Princeton: Princeton University Press, 1990), 67.

35. See Bénédicte Reynaud, *Le Salaire, la règle et le marché* (Paris: Christian Bourgois, 1992), with an introduction by Michel Aglietta. By the same author, see also *Les Théories du salaire*, (Paris: La Découverte, 1994).

36. See Jacques T. Godbout, *The World of the Gift* (Montreal: McGill-Queen's University Press, 1998).

37. As quoted in Jacques T. Godbout, *The World of the Gift*, 79–80.

38. See AA. VV. *Nuove servitù* (Rome: manifestolibri, 1994), and in particular the essay by Marco Bascetta, "L'anima per un salario" and by Franco Carlini, "Professione: accudire il capo."

39. See Karl Marx, *A History of Economic Theories* (New York: Langland Press, 1952).

40. [In English in the original. Trans.]

41. This example was reported in the article "Quality," *Business Week* (August 8, 1994), 40.

42. See Erik Izraelewicz, "L'Amérique sans inflation," *Le Monde* (April 19, 1994).

43. Starting in 1993, the weekly magazine *Business Week* published a long series of articles, analyses and commentaries on noninflationary growth, criticizing the policies of the Federal Reserve. *The Economist*, on the other hand, persists in his monetary approach and tries to insist on the dangers of an "imminent inflation."

44. [Of course, since the 1994 publication of Marazzi's book, Paul Krugman has moved to Princeton, a position as columnist at the *New York Times*, and to winning the 2009 Nobel Prize in economics. Trans.]

45. See Sergio Bologna, "Volare è un po' cadere: I perversi meccanismi della 'deregulation' aerea," *il manifesto* (February 21, 1989).

46. See "The Real Truth about the Economy: Are Government Statistics so much Pulp Fiction?" *Business Week* (November 7, 1994), 44–49.

47. See "The Global Investor: As Foreign Economies Revive, Americans Are Buying Up Overseas Stocks," *Business Week* (September 19, 1994), 40–47.

48. See George Graham, "Haunted by the Specter of Inflation," *Financial Times*, (October 27, 1994), 15. *The Wall Street Journal* aligns itself with the inflationary hypothesis, as shown in the editorial entitled "Taxing to Prosperity" of October 27, 1994. We should remark that in order to be effective in its battle against inflation, the Fed should significantly increase interest rates. But in fact, the growth of the service sector (much less vulnerable to short-term rate increases), the growth in non-banking credit to private firms (as a consequence of the increasingly crucial role played by demand) and economic globalization (and thence the strong presence of foreign investors) are all factors contributing to the weakening of the Fed's role.

49. See "The Information Revolution," *Business Week* (June 13, 1994), 38. For a "map" of investments in the communication network, see "The Global Free-for-All," in *Business Week* (September 26, 1994).

50. See "Trade Tripwires: Tighter Patent and Copyright Laws Will Soon Become Part of Trade Rules," *The Economist* (August 27, 1994).

51. Massimo Cacciari, *Geofilosofia dell'Europa* (Milan: Adelphi, 1994), 168 [our translation].

52. This is the direction indicated in Pierre Maillet and Dario Velo, eds., *L'Europe à géométrie variable: Transition vers l'intégration* (L'Harmattan: Paris, 1994).

2. Rules for the Incommensurable

1. See Alain Bihr, "Crise du sens et tentation autoritaire," *Le Monde Diplomatique* (May 1992), 16–17.

2. [English in original. Trans.]

3. "The World According to Andy Grove," *Business Week* (June 6, 1994), 60–62.

4. See the Introduction, "The Question Then..." in Gilles Deleuze and Félix Guattari, *What Is Philosophy* (New York: Columbia University Press, 1994). We could say that philosophers, in so far as they are "producers of concepts" or "immaterial laborers," share a friendship with their concepts, because the friend is the condition for thinking itself. A philosopher is literally "the *friend* of knowledge."

5. "The World According to Andy Grove," 61.

6. Jean-Claude Kauffmann, *La Trame conjugale: Analyse du couple par son linge* (Paris: Nathan, 1992), 192.

7. Amartya Sen, *Resources, Values, Development* (Oxford: Blackwell, 1984) 371–372. [In this passage, Sen is quoting G. Becker, *A Treatise on the Family* (Cambridge: Harvard University Press, 1981), ix. Trans.]

8. See Marzio Barbagli, *Provando e Riprovando: Matrimonio, famiglia e divorzio in Italia e in altri paesi occidentali* (Bologna: Il Mulino, 1990).

9. On Adam Smith's individuation of the contradiction inherent to the theory of labor value, see Claudio Napoleoni, Valore (Milan: ISEDI, 1976). It should be noted that the first economist who attempted to solve the contradiction between contained and commanded labor was David Ricardo. Marx, on the other hand, supported neither Smith nor Ricardo; instead, he emphasized the contradiction between the two approaches. Smith's approach is considered valid for the explanation of development, Ricardo's for that of exchange as circulation and distribution of goods. According to Marx, there is no solution to this contradiction, because we are dealing with two different qualities of labor: contained labor is dead labor, already performed, while commanded labor is live labor, "subjectivity in action"—labor that has to be commanded in order to function in an economic system where the workers are separated from the means of production.

10. See the important work by Juliet B. Schor, *The Overworked American: the Unexpected Decline of Leisure* (New York: Basic Books, 1993), 1–15. See also Barbagli, 1990, chapter 6.

11. Ida Dominijanni, "La società degli uomini," *il manifesto* (September 13, 1994).

12. [English in original. Trans.]

13. See Jacques Robin, "Mutation technologique, stagnation de la pensée," *Le Monde Diplomatique* (March 1993), 12.

14. On the tautological character of the conventionalist (post-Newtonian and post-Galilean) paradigms of production, see Paolo Virno, *Convenzione e materialismo. L'unicità senza aurea* (Rome and Naples: Theoria, 1986) 37–52.

15. [English in original. Trans.]

16. See Michael Hammer and James Champy, *Reengineering* (Paris: Dunod, 1993) and Franco Carlini "Gli stagionali dei chips: USA, alta tecnologia a bassa occupazione," *il manifesto* (April 6, 1993).

17. See Thomas A. Steward, "Your Company's Most Valuable Asset: Intellectual Capital," *Fortune* (October 1994), 28–33.

18. See Alvin Toffler, *Powershift: Knowledge, Wealth and Violence at the Edge of the 21st Century* (New York: Bantam, 1991), 80–83.

19. See the important study by Charles Goldfinger, *L'Utile et le Futile: L'économie de l'immatériel* (Paris: Odile Jacob, 1994), particularly chapter 4.

20. [English in original. Trans.]

21. [English in original. Trans.]

22. A summary of the study by Helmut Hagmann, director of McKinsey's Munich branch, has been published in *The Wall Street Journal* (October 27, 1994).

23. [English in original. Trans.]

24. [English in original. Trans.]

25. A summary of these theories can be found in the works of Bénédicte Reynaud, *Le Salaire, la règle et le marché* (Paris: Christian Bourgois, 1992), and *Les Théories du salaire* (Paris: La Découverte, 1994).

3. State and Market

[1. Marazzi's skepticism was, of course, more than justified by the events. Hillary Clinton's plan never reached Congress, and sixteen years later economical and political pressures significantly curtailed Obama's reform plans, leading to a botched reform that appears increasingly fragile. Trans.]

2. See the three articles published in *il manifesto* on July 2, 5 and 9, 1992.

3. See "The Global Economy," *The Economist* (October 1, 1994).

4. See Roselyne Pirson, "Surenchère répressive et surveillance des pauvres," *Le Monde diplomatique* (October 1994), 12.

5. See Mariuccia Salvati, "Ceti medi e rappresentanza politica tra storia e sociologia," *Rivista di storia contemporanea* (1988), n. 3.

6. Zygmunt Bauman, *Memories...*, 7.

7. Philip N. Furbank. *Unholy Pleasure, Or the Idea of Social Class* (Oxford: Oxford University Press, 1985), 13.

8. See "Downward Mobility: Corporate Castoffs are struggling just to stay in the Middle-Class," *Business Week*, (March 11, 1992).

9. See Michael W. Horrigan and Steven E. Haugen, "The Declining Middle-Class Thesis: A Sensitivity Analysis," in *Monthly Labor Review* (May 1998).

10. It is important to pause on the increasingly important role played by the entertainment economy, not only from the point of view of job creation, but also as a laboratory for trying out new multimedia technologies. According to an analysis published in *Business Week* (March 14, 1994), the leisure sector has taken the place of the army as the main force driving technological innovation.

11. I am taking this idea from Massimo Cacciari's *DRÂN, Méridiens de la decision dans la pensée contemporaine* (Paris: L'Eclat, 1992), 13. At the beginning of this work, Cacciari quotes Plato: "Don't move what you did not set into place." This is a suggestion that can be quite useful these days. However, for a critique of this politico-analytical line, see Giuseppe Russo, "Idea della politica," *Politica* (Naples: Cronopio, 1993).

12. Alvin Toffler, *Powershift*, 94.

13. Quoted in *il manifesto* (July 9, 1992).

14. The manifesto of the Roman collective "Luogo comune," published in March 1994, reads: "Do you remember the three questions raised by the Abbé Sieyès in his famous pamphlet? 'What is the Third Estate? Everything. What has it been up to now in the political arena? Nothing. What does it want to become? Something.' The Right, presenting itself as a misunderstood and expropriated civil society (although it always had a prominent role in the post–World War Two political ordering) is increasingly adopting the rhetoric of the eighteenth century proponent of bourgeois working ethics. In the 1789 text by Sieyès we are struck by the fact that if we replace 'the privileged' with 'the political class' we find ourselves in the 1990s: 'without any doubt, and because of its idleness, this class is external to the nation.' Thus, the civil society as Third Estate could in fact become a 'free and blossoming Whole' if it could eliminate the privileged political class."

15. See Paul Virilio, *The Art of the Motor*, Minneapolis, University of Minnesota Press, pp. 23 and following. For the following discussion, see the articles on Virilio by Giorgio Boatti, Alberto Abruzzese and Franco Carlini which appeared in *il manifesto*, October 13 1994.

16. See the important study by Daniel Kübler entitled *L'Etat face à la toxicomanie. Action publique et contrat social* (Lausanne: Institut de Sciences Politiques de l'Université de Lausanne, 1993).

17. See Danielle Bütschi and Sandro Cattacin, *Le Modèle Suisse du bien-être* (Lausanne: Réalités sociales, 1994).

18. On this phenomenon, see the enlightening pages by Mike Davis in *City of Quartz: Excavating the Future in Los Angeles* (New York: Routledge, 1990).

19. Giorgio Agamben, "Noi rifugiati," *Luogo comune* (June 1993), 1–4.

Afterword to the Italian Edition

1. [This book, whose title translates as *And So Goes Money: The Financial Market's Exodus and Revolution*, has not yet been translated into English. Trans.]